Extravagant
Hila...

A group of zombies embark on a wife-buying expedition.

Cortés and Montezuma walk together along the docks with gaiety and caution.

Disembodied voices challenge each other to admit their darkest fears.

A man muses on his romance to the tune of a country music version of Mozart's "Abduction from the Seraglio."

The Swedish army maneuvers in Manhattan, encountering some unexpected difficulties.

Books by Donald Barthelme

Amateurs
City Life
The Dead Father
Great Days
Unspeakable Practices, Unnatural Acts

Published by POCKET BOOKS

DONALD BARTHELME

Great Days

PUBLISHED BY POCKET BOOKS NEW YORK

To Thomas B. Hess

All but three of the stories in this book originally appeared in the *New Yorker*.

POCKET BOOKS, a Simon & Schuster division of
GULF & WESTERN CORPORATION
1230 Avenue of the Americas, New York, N.Y. 10020

Published by arrangement with Farrar, Straus & Giroux, Inc.,
Library of Congress Catalog Card Number: 78-10706

ISBN: 0-671-83673-0

First Pocket Books printing July, 1980

10 9 8 7 6 5 4 3 2 1

POCKET and colophon are trademarks of Simon & Schuster.

Printed in the U.S.A.

The Crisis

—On the dedication page of the rebellion, we see the words "To Clementine." A fine sentiment, miscellaneous organ music next, and, turning several pages, massed orange flags at the head of the column. This will not be easy, but neither will it be hard. Good will is everywhere, and the lighthearted song of the gondoliers is heard in the distance.

—Yes, success is everything. Morally important as well as useful in a practical way.

—What have the rebels captured thus far? One zoo, not our best zoo, and a cemetery. The rebels have entered the cages of the tamer animals and are playing with them, gently.

—Things can get better, and in my opinion will.

—Their Graves Registration procedures are scrupulous —accurate and fair.

—There's more to it than playing guitars and clapping

along. Although that frequently gets people in the mood.

—Their methods are direct, not subtle. Dissolution, leaching, sandblasting, cracking and melting of fireproof doors, condemnation, water damage, slide presentations, clamps and buckles.

—And skepticism, although absolutely necessary, leads to not very much.

—The rebels have eaten all the grass on the spacious lawns surrounding the President's heart. That vast organ, the President's heart, beats now on a bald plain.

—It depends on what you want to do. Sometimes people don't know. I mean, don't know even that.

—Clementine is thought to be one of the great rebel leaders of the half century. Her hat has four cockades.

—I loved her for a while. Then, it stopped.

—Rebel T-shirts, camouflaged as ordinary T-shirts by an intense whiteness no eye can pierce, are worn everywhere.

—I don't know why it stopped, it just stopped. That's happened several times. Is something wrong with me?

—Closely supervised voting in the other cantons produced results clearly favorable to neither faction, but rather a sort of generalized approbation which could be appropriated by anyone who had need of it.

—A greater concentration on one person than you normally find. Then, zip.

—Three or four photographs of the rebel generals, tinted glasses, blond locks blowing in the wind, have been released to the world press, in billboard size.

—Whenever I go there, on the Metroliner, I begin quietly thinking about how to help: better planning, more careful management, a more equal distribution of income, education. Or something new.

—There have been mistakes. No attempt was made to seize Broadcasting House—a fundamental error. The Household Cavalry was not subverted, discontented junior officers of the regular forces were not sought out and offered promotions, or money . . .

—Yes, an afternoon on the links! I'd never been out there before—so green and full of holes and flags. I'm afraid we got in the way, people were shouting at us to get out of the way. We had thought they'd let us just stand there and look or walk around and look, but apparently that's not done. So we went to the pro shop and rented some clubs and bags, and put the bags on our shoulders, and that got us by for a while. We walked around with our clubs and bags, enjoying the cool green and the bright, attractive sportswear of the other participants. That helped some, but we were still under some mysterious system of rules we didn't understand, always in the wrong place at the wrong time, it seemed, yelled at and bumping into people. So finally we said to hell with it and left the links; we didn't want to spoil anybody's fun, so we took the bus back to town, first returning the clubs and bags to the pro shop. Next, we will try the jai-alai courts and soccer fields, of which we have heard the most encouraging things.

—Blocking forces were not provided to isolate the Palace. Diversions were not created to draw off key units. The airports were not invested nor were the security services neutralized. Important civilians were not cultivated and won over, and propaganda was neglected. Photographs of the rebel leaders were distributed but these "leaders" were actors, selected for their immense foreheads and chins and blond, flowing locks.

—Yes, they pulled some pretty cute tricks. I had to laugh, sometimes, wondering: What has this to do with you and me? Our frontiers are the marble lobbies of these buildings. True, mortar pits ring the elevator banks but these must be seen as friendly, helpful gestures toward certification of the crisis.

—The present goal of the individual in group enterprises is to avoid dominance; leadership is felt to be a character disorder. Clementine has not heard this news, and thus invariably falls forward, into the thickets of closure.

—Well, maybe so. When I knew her she was just an ordinary woman—wonderful, of course, but not transfigured.

—The black population has steered clear of taking sides, sits home and plays, over and over, the sexy part of *Tristan und Isolde*.

—We feel only 25 percent of what we ought to feel, according to recent findings. I know that "ought" is a loaded word, in this context.

—Are the great bells of the cathedrals an impoverishment of the folk (on one level) or an enrichment of the folk (on another level), and how are these values to be weighted, how reconciled?

—They won't do anything for the poor people, no matter who gets in, and that's a fact. I wonder if they can.

—The raid on the okra fields was not a success; the rebel answering service just hisses.

—There's such a thing as a flash point. But sometimes you can't find it, even when you know how.

—Our pride in having a rebellion of our own, even a faint, rather ill-organized one, has turned us once again toward the kinds of questions that deserve serious attention

—Is something wrong with me? I'm not complaining, just asking. We all have our work, it's the small scale that disturbs. Maybe 25 percent is high. They say he's one of the best, but most people don't need his specialty very often. Of course, I admit that when they need it they need it. Cattle too dream of death, and are afraid of it. I don't mean that as an excuse. I did love her for a while; I remember. His strategy is to be cheerful without being optimistic; I'll go along with that. Maybe we ought to have another election. The police are never happier than on Election Day, when their relation to the citizens assumes a calm, even jokey tone. They are allowed to take off their hats. Fetching coffee in paper cups for the poll watchers, or being fetched coffee by them, they stand chest out not too close to the voting machines in fresh-pressed uniforms, spit-polished boots. Bold sergeants arrive and depart in patrol cars, or dash about making arrangements, and only the plainclothesmen are lonely.

—As a magician works with the unique compressibility of doves, finding some, losing others in the same silk foulard, so the rebels fold scratchy, relaxed meanings into their smallest actions.

—I don't quarrel with their right to do it. It's the means I'm worried about.

—Self-criticism sessions were held, but these produced

more criticism than could usefully be absorbed or accommodated.

—I decided that something is not wrong with me.

—The rebels have failed to make promises. Promises are, perhaps, the nut of the matter. Had they promised everyone free groceries, for example, or one night of love, then their efforts might have—

—Yes, success is everything. Failure is more common. Most achieve a sort of middling thing, but fortunately one's situation is always blurred, you never know absolutely quite where you are. This allows, if not peace of mind, ongoing attention to other aspects of existence.

—But even a poor rebellion has its glorious moments. Let me list some of them. When the flag fell over, and Clem picked it up. When the high priest smeared himself all over with bacon fat and was attacked by red dogs, and Clem scared them off with her bomb. When it was discovered that all of the drumsticks had been left back at the base, and Clem fashioned new ones from ordinary dowels, bought at the hardware store. When gluttons made the line break and waver, and Clem stopped it by stamping her foot, again and again and again.

—When she gets back from the hills, I intend to call her up. It's worth a try.

—Distant fingers from the rebel forces are raised in fond salute.

—The rebel brigades are reading Leskov's *Why Are Books Expensive in Kiev?*

—Three rebellions ago, the air was fresher. The soft pasting noises of the rebel billposters remind us of Oklahoma, where everything is still the same.

The Apology

—Sitting on the floor by the window with only part of my face in the window. He'll never come back.

—Of course he will. He'll return, open the gate with one hand, look up and see your face in the window.

—He'll never come back. Not now.

—He'll come back. New lines on his meager face. Yet with head held high.

—I was unforgivable.

—I would not argue otherwise.

—The black iron gate, difficult to open. Takes two hands. I can see it. It's closed.

—I've had hell with that gate. In winter, without gloves, yanking, late at night, turning my head to see who might be behind me—

—That time that guy was after you—

—The creep—

—With the chain—

—Naw he wasn't the one with the chain he was the other one. With the cudgel.

—Yes they do seem to be carrying cudgels now, I've noticed that. Big knobby cudgels.

—It's a style, makes a statement, something to do with their pricks I imagine.

—Sitting on the floor by the window with only part of my face in the window, the upper part, face truncated under the eyes by the what do you call it, sill.

—But bathed nevertheless by the heat of the fire, which spreads a pleasing warming tickle across your bare back—

—I was unforgivable.

—I don't disagree.

—He'll never come back.

—Say you're sorry.

—I'm not sorry.

—Genuine sorrow is gold. If you can't do it, fake it.

—I'm not sorry.

—Well screw it. It's six of one and half dozen of the other to me. I don't care.

—What?

—Forgive me I didn't mean that.

—What?

—I just meant you could throw him a bone is all I meant. A note written on pale-blue notepaper, in an unsteady hand. "Dear William, it is one of the greatest regrets of my poor life that—"

—Never.

—He may. He might. It's possible. Your position, there in the window, strongly suggests that the affair has yet some energy unexpended. That the magnetic north of your brain may attract his wavering needle still.

—That's kind of you. Kind.

—Your wan, white back. Your green, bifurcated French jeans. Red lines on your back. Cat hair on your jeans.

—Wait. What is it that makes you spring up so, my heart?

—The gate.

—The sound of the gate. The gate opening.

—Is it he?

—It is not. It is someone.

—Let me look.

—He's standing there.

—I know him. Andy deGroot. Looking up at our windows.

—Who's Andy deGroot?

—Guy I know. Melville Fisher Kirkland Leland & deGroot.

—What's he want?

—My devotion. I've disabused him a hundred times, to little avail. If he rings, don't answer. Of course he's more into standing outside and gazing up.

—He looks all right.

—Yes he is all right. That's Andy.

—Powerful forehead on him.

—Yes it is impressive. Stuffed with banana paste.

—Good arms.

—Yes, quite good.

—Looks like he might fly into a rage if crossed.

—He rages constantly.

—We could go out in the street and hit on him, drive him away with blows and imprecations.

—Probably have little or no effect.

—Stick him with the spines of sea urchins.

—Doubt you could penetrate.

—But he's a friend of yours so you say.

—I got no friends babe, no friends, no friends. When you get down to the nut-cutting.

—Go take a poke.

—I don't want to be the first you do it.

—Ah the hell with it. Sitting here with my head hanging in the window, what a way for a grown woman to spend her time.

—Many ways a grown woman can spend her time. Many ways. Lace-making. Feeding the golden carp. Fibonacci numbers.

—Perhaps a new gown, in fawn or taupe. That might be a giggle. Meanwhile, I am planted on this floor. Sitting on the floor by the window with only my great dark eyes visible. My great dark eyes and, in moments of agitation, my great dark nose. Ogled by myriads of citizens bopping down these Chuck's Pizza-plated streets.

—How pale the brow! How pallid the cheek! How chalk the neck! How floury the shoulders! And so on. Say you're sorry.

—I cannot. What's next? Can't sit here all night. I'm nervous. Look on the bright side, maybe he'll go away. He's got a gun stuck in his belt, a belly gun, I saw it. I scraped the oatmeal out of the pot you'll be glad to know. Used the mitt, the black mitt. Throw something at him, a spear or a rock. Open the window first. Spear's in the closet. I can lend you a rock if you don't have a rock. Hurt him. Make him go away. Make the other return. Stir up the fire. Put on some music. Have you no magic? Why do I know you? What are you good for? Why are you here? Fetch me some chocolate? Massage?

—He'll never come back. Until you say it.

—Be damned if I will. Damned a thousand times.

—Then you forfeit the sunshine of his poor blasted face forever. You are dumb, if I may say so, dumb, dumb. It's easy. It's like saying thank you. Myself, I shower thanks everywhere. Thank people for their kindness, thank them for their courtesy. Thank them for their thoughtfulness. Thank them for little things they do if they do little things that are kind, courteous, or thoughtful. Thank them for coming to my house and thank them for leaving. Thank them for what they are about to do as well as thank them for what they have already done, thank them in public and then take them aside privately and thank them again. Thank the thankless and thank the already adequately thanked. In fine, let no occasion pass to slip the chill blade of my thanks between the ribs of every human ear.

—Well. I see what you mean.

—Act.

—Andy has bestirred himself.

—What's he doing?

—Sitting. On a garbage can.

—I knew him long ago, and far away.

—Cincinnati.

—Yes. Engaged then in the manufacture of gearshafts. Had quite a nice wife at that period, name of Caledonia. She split. Then another wife, Cecile as I recall, ran away with a gibbon. Then another wife whose name tax my memory as I may cannot be brought to consciousness, think I spilled something on her once, something that stained. She too evaporated. He came here and joined Melville Fisher etc. Fell in love with a secretary. Polly. She had a beaded curtain in front of her office door and burnt incense. Quite exotic, for Melville Fisher. She ended up in the harem of one of those mystics, a maharooni. Met the old boy once, he grasped my nose and pulled, I felt a great surge of something. Like I was having my nose pulled.

—So that's Andy.

—Yes. What's that sucker doing now?

—He's combing his head. Got him a steel comb, maybe aluminum.

—What's to comb? What's he doing now?

—Adjusting his pants. He's zipping.

—You are aware dear colleague are you not that I cannot abide, cannot abide, even the least wrinkle of vulgarity in social discourse? And that this "zipping" as you call it—

—You are censorious, madame.

—A mere scant shallow preludium, madame, to the remarks I shall bend in your direction should you persist.

—Shall we call the cops?

—And say what?

—Someone's sitting on our garbage can?

—Maybe that's not illegal?

—Oh my God he's got it out in his hands. Oh my God he's pointing his gun at it.

—Oh my God. Shall we call the cops?

—Open the window.

—Open the window?

—Yes open the window.

—Okay the window's open.

—*William! William, wherever you are!*

—You're going to say you're sorry!

—*William! I'm sorry!*

—Andy's put everything away!

—*William I'm sorry I let my brother hoist you up the mast in that crappy jury-rigged bosun's chair while everybody laughed! William I'm sorry I could build better fires than you could! I'm sorry my stack of Christmas cards was always bigger than yours!*

—Andy quails. That's good.

—*William I'm sorry you don't ski and I'm sorry about your back and I'm sorry I invented bop jogging which you couldn't do! I'm sorry I loved Antigua! I'm sorry my mind wandered when you talked about the army! I'm sorry I was superior in argument! I'm sorry you slit open my bicycle tires looking for incriminating letters that you didn't find! You'll never find them!*

—Wow babe that's terrific babe. Very terrific.

—*William! I'm sorry I looked at Sam but he was so handsome, so handsome, who could not! I'm sorry I slept with Sam! I'm sorry about the library books! I'm sorry about Pete! I'm sorry I never played the guitar you gave me! William! I'm sorry I married you and I'll never do it again!*

—Wow.

—Was I sorry enough?

—Well Andy's run away howling.

—Was I sorry enough?

—Terrific. Very terrific.

—Yes I feel much better.

—Didn't I tell you?

—You told me.

—Are you okay?

—Yes I'm fine. Just a little out of breath.

—Well. What's next? Do a little honky-tonking maybe, hit a few bars?

—We could. If you feel like it. Was I sorry enough?

—No.

The New Music

—What did you do today?

—Went to the grocery store and Xeroxed a box of English muffins, two pounds of ground veal and an apple. In flagrant violation of the Copyright Act.

—You had your nap, I remember that—

—I had my nap.

—Lunch, I remember that, there was lunch, slept with Susie after lunch, then your nap, woke up, right?, went Xeroxing, right?, read a book not a whole book but part of a book—

—Talked to Happy on the telephone saw the seven o'clock news did not wash the dishes want to clean up some of this mess?

—If one does nothing but listen to the new music, everything else drifts, goes away, frays. Did Odysseus feel this way when he and Diomedes decided to steal Athene's statue from the Trojans, so that they would become dejected and lose the war? I don't think so, but who is to know what effect the new music of that remote time had on its hearers?

—Or how it compares to the new music of this time?

—One can only conjecture.

—Ah well. I was talking to a girl, talking to her mother actually but the daughter was very much present, on the street. The daughter was absolutely someone you'd like to take to bed and hug and kiss, if you weren't too old. If she weren't too young. She was a wonderful-looking young woman and she was looking at me quite seductively, very seductively, *smoldering* a bit, and I was thinking quite well of myself, very well indeed, thinking myself quite the— Until I realized she was just practicing.

—Yes, I still think of myself as a young man.

—Yes.

—A slightly old young man.

—That's not unusual.

—A slightly old young man still advertising in the trees and rivers for a mate.

—Yes.

—Being clean.

—You're very clean.

—Cleaner than most.

—It's not escaped me. Your cleanness.

—Some of these people aren't clean. People you meet.

—What can you do?

—Set an example. Be clean.

—Dig it, dig it.

—I got three different shower heads. Different degrees of sting.

—Dynamite.

—I got one of these Finnish pads that slip over the hand.

—*Numero uno.*

—Pedicare. That's another thing.

—Think you're the mule's eyebrows don't you?

—No. I feel like Insufficient Funds.

—Feel like a busted-up car by the side of the road stripped of value.

—Feel like *I don't like this!*

—You're just a little down, man, down, that's what they call it, down.

—Well how come they didn't bring us no ring of roses with a purple silk sash with gold lettering on that mother? How come that?

—Dunno baby. Maybe we lost?

—How could we lose? How could we? We!

—We were standing tall. Ready to hand them their asses, clean their clocks. Yet maybe—

—I remember the old days when we almost automatically—

—Yes. Almost without effort—

—Right. Come in, Commander. Put it right there, anywhere will do, let me move that for you. Just put that sucker down right there. An eleven-foot-high silver cup!

—Beautifully engraved, with dates.

—Beautifully engraved, with dates. That was then.

—Well. Is there help coming?

—I called the number for help and they said there was no more help.

—I'm taking you to Pool.

—I've been there.

—I'm taking you to Pool, city of new life.

—Maybe tomorrow or another day.

—Pool, the revivifier.

—Oh man I'm not up for it.

—Where one can taste the essences, get swindled into health.

—I got things to do.

—That lonesome road. It ends in Pool.

—Got to chop a little cotton, go by the drugstore.

—Ever been to Pool?

—Yes I've been there.

—Pool, city of new hope.

—Get my ocarina tuned, sew a button on my shirt.

—Have you traveled much? Have you traveled enough?

—I've traveled a bit.

—Got to go away 'fore you can get back, that's fundamental.

—The joy of return is my joy. Satisfied by a walk around the block.

—Pool. Have you seen the new barracks? For the State Police? They used that red rock they have around there, quite a handsome structure, dim and red.

—Do the cops like it?

—No one has asked them. But they could hardly . . . I mean it's new.

—Got to air my sleeping bag, scrub up my canteen.

—Have you seen the new amphitheater? Made out of red rock. They play all the tragedies.

—Yeah I've seen it that's over by the train station right?

—No it's closer to the Great Lyceum. The Great Lyceum glowing like an ember against the hubris of the city.

—I could certainly use some home fries 'long about now. Home fries and ketchup.

—Pool. The idea was that it be one of those new towns. Where everyone would be happier. The regulations are quite strict. They don't let people have cars.

—Yes, I was in on the beginning. I remember the charette, I was asked to prepare a paper. But I couldn't think of anything. I stood there wearing this blue smock stenciled with the Pool emblem, looked rather like a maternity gown. I couldn't think of anything to say. Finally I said I would go along with the group.

—The only thing old there is the monastery, dates from 1720 or thereabouts. Has the Dark Virgin, the Virgin is black, as is the Child. Dates from 1720 or around in there.

—I've seen it. Rich fare, extraordinarily rich, makes you want to cry.

—And in the fall the circus comes. Plays the red rock gardens where the carved red asters, carved red phlox, are set off by borders of yellow beryl.

—I've seen it. Extraordinarily rich.

—So it's settled, we'll go to Pool, there'll be routs and revels, maybe a sock hop, maybe a nuzzle or two on the terrace with one of the dazzling Pool beauties—

—Not much for nuzzling, now. I mostly kneel at their feet, knit for them or parse for them—

—And the Pool buffalo herd. Six thousand beasts. All still alive.

—Each house has its grand lawns and grounds, brass candlesticks, thrice-daily mail delivery. Elegant widowed women living alone in large houses, watering lawns with whirling yellow sprinklers, studying the patterns of the grass, searching out brown patches to be sprinkled. Sometimes there is a grown child in the house, or an almost-grown one, working for a school or hospital in a teaching or counseling position. Frequently there are family photographs on the walls of the house, about which you are encouraged to ask questions. At dusk medals are awarded those who have made it through the day, the Cross of St. Jaime, the Cross of St. Em.

—Meant to be one of those new towns where everyone would be happier, much happier, that was the idea.

—Serenity. Peace. The dead are shown in art galleries, framed. Or sometimes, put on pedestals. Not much different from the practice elsewhere except that in Pool they display the actual—

—Person.

—Yes.

—And they play a tape of the guy or woman talking, right next to his or her—

—Frame or pedestal.

—Prerecorded.

—Naturally.

—Shocked white faces talking.

—Killed a few flowers and put them in pots under the faces, everybody does that.

—Something keeps drawing you back like a magnet.

—Watching the buffalo graze. It can't be this that I've waited for, I've waited too long. I find it intolerable, all this putter. Yet in the end, wouldn't mind doing a little grazing myself, it would look a little funny.

—Is there bluegrass in heaven? Make inquiries. I saw the streets of Pool, a few curs broiling on spits.

—And on another corner, a man spinning a goat into gold.

—Pool projects positive images of itself through the great medium of film.

—Cinemas filled with industrious product.

—Real films. Sent everywhere.

—Film is the great medium of this century—hearty, giggling film.

—So even if one does not go there, one may assimilate the meaning of Pool.

—I'd just like to rest and laze around.

—Soundtracks in Burmese, Italian, Twi, and other tongues.

—One film is worth a thousand words. At least a thousand.

—There's a film about the new barracks, and a film about the new amphitheater.

—Good. Excellent.

—In the one about the new barracks we see Squadron A at morning roll call, tense and efficient. "Mattingly!" calls the sergeant. "Yo!" says Mattingly. "Morgan!" calls the sergeant. "Yo!" says Morgan.

—A fine bunch of men. Nervous, but fine.

—In the one about the amphitheater, an eight-day dramatization of Eckermann's *Conversations with Goethe*.

—What does Goethe say?

—Goethe says: "I have devoted my whole life to the people and their improvement."

—Goethe said that?

—And is quoted in the very superior Pool production which is enlustering the perception of Pool worldwide.

—Rich, very rich.

—And there is a film chronicling the fabulous Pool garage sales, where one finds solid-silver plates in neglected bags.

—People sighing and leaning against each other, holding their silver plates. Think I'll just whittle a bit, whittle and spit.

—Lots of accommodations in Pool, all of the hotels are empty.

—See if I have any benefits left under the G.I. Bill.

—Pool is new, can make you new too.

—I have not the heart.

—I can get us a plane or a train, they've cut all the fares.

—People sighing and leaning against one another, holding their silver plates.

—So you just want to stay here? Stay here and be yourself?

—Drop by the shoe store, pick up a pair of shoes.

—Blackberries, buttercups, and wild red clover. I find the latest music terrific, although I don't generally speaking care much for the new, qua new. But this new music! It has won from our group the steadiest attention.

—Momma didn't 'low no clarinet played in here. Unfortunately.

—Momma.

—Momma didn't 'low no clarinet played in here. Made me sad.

—Momma was outside.

—Momma was *very* outside.

—Sitting there 'lowing and not-'lowing. In her old rocking chair.

—'Lowing this, not-'lowing that.

—Didn't 'low oboe.

—Didn't 'low gitfiddle. Vibes.

—Rock over your damn foot and bust it, you didn't pop to when she was 'lowing and not-'lowing.

—Right. 'Course, she had all the grease.

—True.

—You wanted a little grease, like to buy a damn comic book or something, you had to go to Momma.

—Sometimes yes, sometimes no. Her variously colored moods.

—Mauve. Warm gold. Citizen's blue.

—Mauve mood that got her thrown in the jug that time.

—Concealed weapons. Well, what can you do?

—Carried a .357 daytimes and a .22 for evenings. Well, what can you do?

—Momma didn't let nobody work her over, nobody.

—She just didn't give a hang. She didn't care.

—I thought she cared. There were moments.

—She never cared. Didn't give pig shit.

—You could even cry, she wouldn't come.

—I tried that, I remember. Cried and cried. Didn't do a damn bit of good.

—Lost as she was in the Eleusinian mysteries and the art of love.

—Cried my little eyes out. The sheet was sopping.

—Momma was not to be swayed. Unswayable.

—Staring into the thermostat.

—She had a lot on her mind. The chants. And Daddy, of course.

—Let's not do Daddy today.

—Yes, I remember Momma, jerking the old nervous system about with her electric *diktats*.

—Could Christ have performed the work of the Redemption had He come into the world in the shape of a pea? That was one she'd drop on you.

—Then she'd grade your paper.

—I got a C, once.

—She dyed my beard blue, on the eve of my seventh marriage. I was sleeping on the sun porch.

—Not one to withhold comment, Momma.

—Got pretty damned tired of that old woman, pretty damned tired of that old woman. Gangs of ecstatics hanging about beating on pots and pans, trash-can lids—

—Trying for a ticket to the mysteries.

—You wanted a little grease, like to go to the brothel or something, you had to say, Momma can I have a little grease to go to the brothel?

—She was often underly generous.

—Give you eight when she knew it was ten.

—She had her up days and her down days. Like most.

—Out for a long walk one early evening I noticed in the bare brown cut fields to the right of me and to the left of me the following items of interest: in the field to the right of me, couple copulating in the shade of a car, tan Studebaker as I remember, a thing I had seen previously only in old sepia-toned photographs taken from the air by playful barnstormers capable of flying with their knees, I don't know if that's difficult or not—

—And in the field to your left?

—Momma. Rocking.

—She'd lugged the old rocking chair all that way. In a mauve mood.

—I tipped my hat. She did not return the greeting.

—She was pondering. "The goddess Demeter's anguish for all her children's mortality."

—Said my discourse was sickening. That was the word she used. Said it repeatedly.

—I asked myself: Do I give a bag of beans?

—This bird that fell into the back yard?

—The south lawn.

—The back yard. I wanted to give it a Frito?

—Yeah?

—Thought it might be hungry. Sumbitch couldn't fly you understand. It had crashed. Couldn't fly. So I went into the house to get it a Frito. So I was trying to get it to eat the Frito. I had the damn bird in one hand, and in the other, the Frito.

—She saw you and whopped you.

—She did.

—She gave you that "the bird is our friend and we never touch the bird because it hurts the bird" number.

—She did.

—Then she threw the bird away.

—Into the gutter.

—Anticipating no doubt handling of the matter by the proper authorities.

—Momma. You'd ask her how she was and she'd say, "Fine." Like a little kid.

—That's what they say. "Fine."

—That's all you can get out of 'em. "Fine."

—Boy or girl, don't make a penny's worth of difference. "Fine."

—Fending you off. Similarly, Momma.

—Momma 'lowed lute.

—Yes. She had a thing for lute.

—I remember the hours we spent. Banging away at our lutes.

—Momma sitting there rocking away. Dosing herself with strange intoxicants.

—Lime Rickeys.

—Orange Blossoms.

—Rob Roys.

—Cuba Libres.

—Brandy Alexanders and Bronxes. How could she drink that stuff?

—An iron gut. And divinity, of course.

—Well. Want to clean up some of this mess?

—Some monster with claws, maybe velvet-covered claws or Teflon-covered claws, inhabits my dreams. Whistling, whistling. I say, Monster, how goes it with you? And he says, Quite happily, dreammate, there are certain criticisms, the Curator of Archetypes thinks I don't quite cut it, thinks I'm shuckin' and jivin' when what I should be doing is attacking, attacking, attacking—

—Ah, my bawcock, what a fine fellow thou art.

—*But on the whole,* the monster says, I feel fine. Then he says, Gimme that corn flake back. I say, What? He says, Gimme that corn flake back. I say, You gave me that corn flake it's my corn flake. He says, Gimme that corn flake back or I'll claw you to thread. I say, I can't man you gave it to me I already ate it. He says, C'mon man gimme the corn flake back did you butter it first? I say, C'mon man be reasonable, you don't butter a corn flake—

—How does it end?

—It doesn't end.

—Is there help coming?

—I called that number and they said whom the Lord loveth He chasteneth.

—Where is succor?

—In the new music.

—Yes, it isn't often you hear a disco version of *Un Coup de Dés.* It's strengthening.

—The new music is drumless, which is brave. To make up for the absence of drums the musicians pray nightly to the Virgin, kneeling in their suits of lights in damp chapels provided for the purpose off the corridors of the great arenas—

—Momma wouldn't have 'lowed it.

—As with much else. Momma didn't 'low Patrice.

—I remember. You still see her?

—Once in a way. Saw her Saturday. I hugged her and her body leaped. That was odd.

—How did that feel?

—Odd. Wonderful.

—The body knows.

—The body is perspicacious.

—The body ain't dumb.

—Words can't say what the body knows.

—Sometimes I hear them howling from the hospital.

—The detox ward.

—Tied to the bed with beige cloths.

—We've avoided it.

—So far.

—Knock wood.

—I did.

—Well, it's a bitch.

—Like when she played Scrabble. She played to kill. Used the filthiest words insisting on their legitimacy. I was shocked.

—In her robes of deep purple.

—Seeking the ecstatic vision. That which would lift people four feet off the floor.

—Six feet.

—Four feet or six feet off the floor. Persephone herself appearing.

—The chanting in the darkened telesterion.

—Persephone herself appearing, hovering. Accepting

offerings, balls of salt, solid gold serpents, fig branches, figs.

—Hallucinatory dancing. All the women drunk.

—Dancing with jugs on their heads, mixtures of barley, water, mint—

—Knowledge of things unspeakable—

—Still, all I wanted to do was a little krummhorn. A little krummhorn once in a while.

—Can open graves, properly played.

—I was never good. Never really good.

—Who could practice?

—And your clavier.

—Momma didn't 'low clavier.

—Thought it would unleash in her impulses better leashed? I don't know.

—Her dark side. They all have them, mommas.

—I mean they've seen it all, felt it all. Spilled their damn blood and then spooned out buckets of mushy squash meanwhile telling the old husband that he wasn't number three on the scale of all husbands . . .

—Tossed him a little bombita now and then just to keep him on his toes.

—He was always on his toes, spent his whole life on his toes, the poor fuck. Piling up the grease.

—We said we weren't going to do Daddy.

—I forgot.

—Old Momma.

—Well, it's not easy, conducting the mysteries. It's not easy, making the corn grow.

—Asparagus too.

—I couldn't do it.

—I couldn't do it.

—Momma could do it.

—Momma.

—Luckily we have the new music now. To give us aid and comfort.

—And Susie.

—Our Susie.

—Our darling.

—Our pride.

—Our passion.

—I have to tell you something. Susie's been reading the Hite Report. She says other women have more orgasms than she does. Wanted to know why.

—Where does one go to complain? Where does one go to complain, when fiends have worsened your life?

—I told her about the Great Septuagesimal Orgasm, implying she could have one, if she was good. But it is growing late, very late indeed, for such as we.

—But perhaps one ought *not* to complain, when fiends have worsened your life. But rather, emulating the great Stoics, Epictetus and so on, just zip into a bar and lift a few, whilst listening to the new, incorrigible, great-white-shark, knife, music.

—I handed the tall cool Shirley Temple to the silent priest. The new music, I said, is not specifically anticlerical. Only in its deepest effects.

—I know the guy who plays washboard. Wears thimbles on all his fingers.

—The new music burns things together, like a welder.

The new music says, life becomes more and more exciting as there is less and less time.

—Momma wouldn't have 'lowed it. But Momma's gone.

—To the curious: A man who was a Communist heard the new music, and now is not. Fernando the fish-seller was taught to read and write by the new music, and is now a leper, white as snow. William Friend was caught trying to sneak into the new music with a set of bongos concealed under his cloak, but was garroted with his own bicycle chain, just in time. Propp the philosopher, having dinner with the Holy Ghost, was told of the coming of the new music but also informed that he would not live to hear it.

—The new, down-to-earth, think-I'm-gonna-kill-myself music, which unwraps the sky.

—Succeed! It has been done, and with a stupidity that can astound the most experienced.

—The rest of the trip presents no real difficulties.

—The rest of the trip presents no real difficulties. The thing to keep your eye on is less time, more exciting. Remember that.

—As if it were late, late, and we were ready to pull on our red-and-gold-striped nightshirts.

—Cup of tea before retiring.

—Cup of tea before retiring.

—Dreams next.

—We can deal with that.

—Remembering that the new music will be there tomorrow and tomorrow and tomorrow.

—There is always a new music.

—Thank God.

—Pull a few hairs out of your nose poised before the mirror.

—Routine maintenance, nothing to write home about.

Cortés
and Montezuma

Because Cortés lands on a day specified in the ancient writings, because he is dressed in black, because his armor is silver in color, a certain *ugliness* of the strangers taken as a group—for these reasons, Montezuma considers Cortés to be Quetzalcoatl, the great god who left Mexico many years before, on a raft of snakes, vowing to return.

Montezuma gives Cortés a carved jade drinking cup.

Cortés places around Montezuma's neck a necklace of glass beads strung on a cord scented with musk.

Montezuma offers Cortés an earthenware platter containing small pieces of meat lightly breaded and browned which Cortés declines because he knows the small pieces of meat are human fingers.

Cortés sends Montezuma a huge basket of that Spanish bread of which Montezuma's messengers had said, on first encountering the Spaniards, "As to their food, it is like human food, it is white and not heavy, and slightly sweet . . ."

Cortés and Montezuma are walking, down by the docks. Little green flies fill the air. Cortés and Montezuma are holding hands; from time to time one of them disengages a hand to brush away a fly.

Montezuma receives new messages, in picture writing, from the hills. These he burns, so that Cortés will not learn their contents. Cortés is trimming his black beard.

Doña Marina, the Indian translator, is sleeping with Cortés in the palace given him by Montezuma. Cortés awakens; they share a cup of chocolate. *She looks tired*, Cortés thinks.

Down by the docks, Cortés and Montezuma walk, holding hands. "Are you acquainted with a Father Sanchez?" Montezuma asks. "Sanchez, yes, what's he been up to?" says Cortés. "Overturning idols," says Montezuma. "Yes," Cortés says vaguely, "yes, he does that, everywhere we go."

At a concert later that evening, Cortés is bitten on the ankle by a green insect. The bug crawls into his velvet slipper. Cortés removes the slipper, feels around inside, finds the bug and removes it. "Is this poisonous?" he asks Doña Marina. "Perfectly," she says.

Montezuma himself performs the operation upon Cortés's swollen ankle. He lances the bitten place with a sharp knife, then sucks the poison from the wound, spits. Soon they are walking again, down by the docks.

Montezuma writes, in a letter to his mother: "The new forwardness of the nobility has come as a welcome relief. Whereas formerly members of the nobility took pains to hide among the general population, to pretend that they were ordinary people, they are now flaunting themselves and their position in the most disgusting ways. Once again they wear scarlet sashes from shoulder to hip, even on the boulevards; once again they prance about in their great powdered wigs; once again they employ lackeys to stand in pairs on little shelves at the rear of their limousines. The din raised by their incessant visiting of one another is with us from noon until early in the morning . . .

"This flagrant behavior is, as I say, welcome. For we are all tired of having to deal with their manifold deceptions, of uncovering their places of concealment, of keeping track of their movements—in short, of having to think about them, of having to *remember* them. Their new assertiveness, however much it reminds us of the excesses of former times, is easier. The interesting question is, what has emboldened the nobility to emerge from obscurity at this time? Why now?

"Many people here are of the opinion that it is a direct consequence of the plague of devils we have had recently. It is easily seen that, against a horizon of devils, the reappearance of the nobility can only be considered a more or less tolerable circumstance—they themselves must have realized this. Not since the late years of the last Bundle have we had so many spitting, farting, hair-shedding devils abroad. Along with the devils there have been roaches, roaches big as ironing boards. Then, too, we have the Spaniards . . ."

A group of great lords hostile to Montezuma holds a secret meeting in Vera Cruz, under the special protection of the god Smoking Mirror. Debate is fierce; a heavy rain is falling; new arrivals crowd the room.

Doña Marina, although she is the mistress of Cortés, has an Indian lover of high rank as well. Making her confession to Father Sanchez, she touches upon this. "His name is Cuitlahuac? This may be useful politically. I cannot give you absolution, but I will remember you in my prayers."

In the gardens of Tenochtitlán, whisperers exchange strange new words: *guillotine, white pepper, sincerity, temperament.*

Cortés's men break through many more walls but behind these walls they find, invariably, only the mummified carcasses of dogs, cats, and sacred birds.

Down by the docks, Cortés and Montezuma walk, holding hands. Cortés has employed a detective to follow Montezuma; Montezuma has employed a detective to follow Father Sanchez. "There are only five detectives of talent in Tenochtitlán," says Montezuma. "There are others, but I don't use them. Visions are best—better than the best detective."

Atop the great Cue, or pyramid, Cortés strikes an effigy of the god Blue Hummingbird and knocks off its golden mask; an image of the Virgin is installed in its place.

"The heads of the Spaniards," says Doña Marina, "Juan de Escalante and the five others, were arranged in a row on a pike. The heads of their horses were arranged in another row on another pike, set beneath the first."

Cortés screams.

The guards run in, first Cristóbal de Olid, and following him Pedro de Alvarado and then de Ordás and de Tapia.

Cortés is raving. He runs from the palace into the plaza where he meets and is greeted by Montezuma. Two great lords stand on either side of Montezuma supporting his arms, which are spread wide in greeting. They fold Montezuma's arms around Cortés. Cortés speaks urgently into Montezuma's ear.

Montezuma removes from his bosom a long cactus thorn and pricks his ear with it repeatedly, until the blood flows.

Doña Marina is walking, down by the docks, with her lover Cuitlahuac, Lord of the Place of the Dunged Water. "When I was young," says Cuitlahuac, "I was at school with Montezuma. He was, in contrast to the rest of us, remarkably chaste. A very religious man, a great student— I'll wager that's what they talk about, Montezuma and

Cortés. Theology." Doña Marina tucks a hand inside his belt, at the back.

Bernal Diaz del Castillo, who will one day write *The True History of the Conquest of New Spain*, stands in a square whittling upon a piece of mesquite. The Proclamation of Vera Cruz is read, in which the friendship of Cortés and Montezuma is denounced as contrary to the best interests of the people of Mexico, born and yet unborn.

Cortés and Montezuma are walking, down by the docks. "I especially like the Holy Ghost. Qua idea," says Montezuma. "The other God, the Father, is also—" "One God, three Persons," Cortés corrects gently. "That the Son should be sacrificed," Montezuma continues, "seems to me wrong. It seems to me He should be sacrificed *to*. Furthermore," Montezuma stops and taps Cortés meaningfully on the chest with a brown forefinger, "where is the Mother?"

Bernal asks Montezuma, as a great favor, for a young pretty woman; Montezuma sends him a young woman of good family, together with a featherwork mantle, some crickets in cages, and a quantity of freshly made soap. Montezuma observes, of Bernal, that "he seems to be a gentleman."

"The ruler prepares dramas for the people," Montezuma says.

Cortés, sitting in an armchair, nods.

"Because the cultivation of maize requires on the average only fifty days' labor per person per year, the people's energies may be invested in these dramas—for example the eternal struggle to win, to retain, the good will of Smoking Mirror, Blue Hummingbird, Quetzalcoatl . . ."

Cortés smiles and bows.

"Easing the psychological strain on the ruler who would otherwise be forced to face alone the prospect of world collapse, the prospect of the world folding in on itself . . ."

Cortés blinks.

"If the drama is not of my authorship, if events are not controllable by me—"

Cortés has no reply.

"Therefore it is incumbent upon you, dear brother, to disclose to me the ending or at least what you know of the drama's probable course so that I may attempt to manipulate it in a favorable direction with the application of what magic is left to me."

Cortés has no reply.

Breaking through a new wall, Cortés's men discover, on the floor of a chamber behind the wall, a tiny puddle of gold. The Proclamation is circulated throughout the city; is sent to other cities.

Bernal builds a stout hen coop for Doña Marina. The sky over Tenochtitlán darkens; flashes of lightning; then rain sweeping off the lake.

Down by the docks, Cortés and Montezuma take shelter in a doorway. "Doña Marina translated it; I have a copy," says Cortés.

"When you smashed Blue Hummingbird with the crowbar—"

"I was rash. I admit it."

"You may take the gold with you. All of it. My gift."

"Your Highness is most kind."

"Your ships are ready. My messengers say their sails are as many as the clouds over the water."

"I cannot leave until all of the gold in Mexico, past, present and future, is stacked in the holds."

"Impossible on the face of it."

"I agree. Let us talk of something else."

Montezuma notices that a certain amount of white lint has accumulated on his friend's black velvet doublet. He thinks: *She should take better care of him.*

In bed with Cortés, Doña Marina displays for his eyes her beautiful golden buttocks, which he strokes reverently. A tiny green fly is buzzing about the room; Cortés brushes it away with a fly whisk made of golden wire. She tells him about a vision. In the vision Montezuma is struck in the forehead by a large stone, and falls. His enraged subjects hurl more stones.

"Don't worry," says Cortés. "Trust me."

Father Sanchez confronts Cortés with the report of the detective he has hired to follow Doña Marina, together with other reports, documents, photographs. Cortés orders that all of the detectives in the city be arrested, that the profession of detective be abolished forever in Tenochtitlán, and that Father Sanchez be sent back to Cuba in chains.

In the marketplaces and theaters of the city, new words are passed about: *tranquillity, vinegar, entitlement, schnell.*

On another day Montezuma and Cortés and Doña Marina and the guard of Cortés and certain great lords of Tenochtitlán leave their palaces and are carried in palanquins to the part of the city called Cotaxtla.

There, they halt before a great house and dismount.

"What is this place?" Cortés asks, for he has never seen it before.

Montezuma replies that it is the meeting place of the Aztec council or legislature which formulates the laws of his people.

Cortés expresses surprise and states that it had been his understanding that Montezuma is an absolute ruler answerable to no one—a statement Doña Marina tactfully neglects to translate lest Montezuma be given offense by it.

Cortés, with his guard at his back and Montezuma at his right hand, enters the building.

At the end of a long hallway he sees a group of functionaries each of whom wears in his ears long white goose quills filled with powdered gold. Here Cortés and his men are fumigated with incense from large pottery braziers, but Montezuma is not, the major-domos fix their eyes on the ground and do not look at him but greet him with great reverence saying, "Lord, my Lord, my Great Lord."

The party is ushered through a pair of tall doors of fragrant cedar into a vast chamber hung with red and yellow banners. There, on low wooden benches divided by a broad aisle, sit the members of the council, facing a dais. There are perhaps three hundred of them, each wearing affixed to his buttocks a pair of mirrors as is appropriate to his rank. On the dais are three figures of considerable majesty, the one in the center raised somewhat above his fellows; behind them, on the wall, hangs a great wheel of gold with much intricate featherwork depicting a whirlpool with the features of the goddess Chalchihuitlicue in the center. The council members sit in attitudes of rigid attention, arms held at their sides, chins lifted, eyes fixed on the dais. Cortés lays a hand on the shoulder of one of them, then recoils. He raps with his knuckles on that shoulder which gives forth a hollow sound. "They are pottery," he says to Montezuma. Montezuma winks. Cortés begins to laugh. Montezuma begins to laugh. Cortés is choking, hysterical. Cortés and Montezuma run around the great hall, dodging in and out of the rows of benches, jumping into the laps of one or another of the clay figures, overturning some, turning others backwards in their seats. "I am the State!" shouts Montezuma, and Cortés shouts, "Mother of God, forgive this poor fool who doesn't know what he is saying!"

In the kindest possible way, Cortés places Montezuma under house arrest.

"Best you come to stay with me a while."

"Thank you but I'd rather not."

"We'll have games and in the evenings, home movies."

"The people wouldn't understand."

"We've got Pitalpitoque shackled to the great chain."

"I thought it was Quintalbor."

"Pitalpitoque, Quintalbor, Tendile."

"I'll send them chocolate."

"Come away, come away, come away with me."

"The people will be frightened."

"What do the omens say?"

"I don't know I can't read them any more."

"Cutting people's hearts out, forty, fifty, sixty at a crack."

"It's the custom around here."

"The people of the South say you take too much tribute."

"Can't run an empire without tribute."

"Our Lord Jesus Christ loves you."

"I'll send Him chocolate."

"Come away, come away, come away with me."

Down by the docks, Cortés and Montezuma are walking with Charles V, Emperor of Spain. Doña Marina follows at a respectful distance carrying two picnic baskets containing many delicacies: caviar, white wine, stuffed thrushes, gumbo.

Charles V bends to hear what Montezuma is saying; Cortés brushes from the person of the Emperor little green flies, using a fly whisk made of golden wire. "Was there no alternative?" Charles asks. "I did what I thought best," says Cortés, "proceeding with gaiety and conscience." "I am murdered," says Montezuma.

The sky over Tenochtitlán darkens; flashes of lightning; then rain sweeping off the lake.

The pair walking down by the docks, hand in hand, the ghost of Montezuma rebukes the ghost of Cortés. "Why did you not throw up your hand, and catch the stone?"

The King of Jazz

Well I'm the king of jazz now, thought Hokie Mokie to himself as he oiled the slide on his trombone. Hasn't been a 'bone man been king of jazz 'or many years. But now that Spicy MacLammermoor, the old king, is dead, I guess I'm it. Maybe I better play a few notes out of this window here, to reassure myself.

"Wow!" said somebody standing on the sidewalk. "Did you hear that?"

"I did," said his companion.

"Can you distinguish our great homemade American jazz performers, each from the other?"

"Used to could."

"Then who was that playing?"

"Sounds like Hokie Mokie to me. Those few but perfectly selected notes have the real epiphanic glow."

"The what?"

"The real epiphanic glow, such as is obtained only by artists of the caliber of Hokie Mokie, who's from Pass Christian, Mississippi. He's the king of jazz, now that Spicy MacLammermoor is gone."

Hokie Mokie put his trombone in its trombone case and went to a gig. At the gig everyone fell back before him, bowing.

"Hi Bucky! Hi Zoot! Hi Freddie! Hi George! Hi Thad! Hi Roy! Hi Dexter! Hi Jo! Hi Willie! Hi Greens!"

"What we gonna play, Hokie? You the king of jazz now, you gotta decide."

"How 'bout 'Smoke'?"

"Wow!" everybody said. "Did you hear that? Hokie Mokie can just knock a fella out, just the way he pronounces a word. What a intonation on that boy! God Almighty!"

"I don't want to play 'Smoke,' " somebody said.

"Would you repeat that, stranger?"

"I don't want to play 'Smoke.' 'Smoke' is dull. I don't like the changes. I refuse to play 'Smoke.' "

"He refuses to play 'Smoke'! But Hokie Mokie is the king of jazz and he says 'Smoke'!"

"Man, you from outa town or something? What do you mean you refuse to play 'Smoke'? How'd you get on this gig anyhow? Who hired you?"

"I am Hideo Yamaguchi, from Tokyo, Japan."

"Oh, you're one of those Japanese cats, eh?"

"Yes I'm the top trombone man in all of Japan."

"Well you're welcome here until we hear you play. Tell

me, is the Tennessee Tea Room still the top jazz place in Tokyo?"

"No, the top jazz place in Tokyo is the Square Box now."

"That's nice. O.K., now we gonna play 'Smoke' just like Hokie said. You ready, Hokie? O.K., give you four for nothin'. One! Two! Three! Four!"

The two men who had been standing under Hokie's window had followed him to the club. Now they said:

"Good God!"

"Yes, that's Hokie's famous 'English sunrise' way of playing. Playing with lots of rays coming out of it, some red rays, some blue rays, some green rays, some green stemming from a violet center, some olive stemming from a tan center—"

"That young Japanese fellow is pretty good, too."

"Yes, he is pretty good. And he holds his horn in a peculiar way. That's frequently the mark of a superior player."

"Bent over like that with his head between his knees— good God, he's sensational!"

He's sensational, Hokie thought. Maybe I ought to kill him.

But at that moment somebody came in the door pushing in front of him a four-and-one-half-octave marimba. Yes, it was Fat Man Jones, and he began to play even before he was fully in the door.

"What're we playing?"

" 'Billie's Bounce.' "

"That's what I thought it was. What're we in?"

"F."

"That's what I thought we were in. Didn't you use to play with Maynard?"

"Yeah I was on that band for a while until I was in the hospital."

"What for?"

"I was tired."

"What can we add to Hokie's fantastic playing?"

"How 'bout some rain or stars?"

"Maybe that's presumptuous?"

"Ask him if he'd mind."

"You ask him, I'm scared. You don't fool around with the king of jazz. That young Japanese guy's pretty good, too."

"He's sensational."

"You think he's playing in Japanese?"

"Well I don't think it's English."

This trombone's been makin' my neck green for thirty-five years, Hokie thought. How come I got to stand up to yet another challenge, this late in life?

"Well, Hideo—"

"Yes, Mr. Mokie?"

"You did well on both 'Smoke' and 'Billie's Bounce.' You're just about as good as me, I regret to say. In fact, I've decided you're *better* than me. It's a hideous thing to contemplate, but there it is. I have only been the king of jazz for twenty-four hours, but the unforgiving logic of this art demands we bow to Truth, when we hear it."

"Maybe you're mistaken?"

"No, I got ears. I'm not mistaken. Hideo Yamaguchi is the new king of jazz."

"You want to be king emeritus?"

"No, I'm just going to fold up my horn and steal away. This gig is yours, Hideo. You can pick the next tune."

"How 'bout 'Cream'?"

"O.K., you heard what Hideo said, it's 'Cream.' You ready, Hideo?"

"Hokie, you don't have to leave. You can play too. Just move a little over to the side there—"

"Thank you, Hideo, that's very gracious of you. I guess I will play a little, since I'm still here. Sotto voce, of course."

"Hideo is wonderful on 'Cream'!"

"Yes, I imagine it's his best tune."

"What's that sound coming in from the side there?"

"Which side?"

"The left."

"You mean that sound that sounds like the cutting edge of life? That sounds like polar bears crossing Arctic ice pans? That sounds like a herd of musk ox in full flight? That sounds like male walruses diving to the bottom of the sea? That sounds like fumaroles smoking on the slopes of Mt. Katmai? That sounds like the wild turkey walking through the deep, soft forest? That sounds like beavers chewing trees in an Appalachian marsh? That sounds like an oyster fungus growing on an aspen trunk? That sounds like a mule deer wandering a montane of the Sierra Nevada? That sounds like prairie dogs kissing? That sounds like witchgrass tumbling or a river meandering? That sounds like manatees munching seaweed at Cape Sable? That sounds like coatimundis moving in packs across the face of Arkansas? That sounds like—"

"Good God, it's Hokie! Even with a cup mute on, he's blowing Hideo right off the stand!"

"Hideo's playing on his knees now! Good God, he's reaching into his belt for a large steel sword— Stop him!"

"Wow! That was the most exciting 'Cream' ever played! Is Hideo all right?"

"Yes, somebody is getting him a glass of water."

"You're my man, Hokie! That was the dadblangedest thing I ever saw!"

"You're the king of jazz once again!"

"Hokie Mokie is the most happening thing there is!"

"Yes, Mr. Hokie sir, I have to admit it, you blew me right off the stand. I see I have many years of work and study before me still."

"That's O.K., son. Don't think a thing about it. It happens to the best of us. Or it almost happens to the best of us. Now I want everybody to have a good time because we're gonna play 'Flats.' 'Flats' is next."

"With your permission, sir, I will return to my hotel and pack. I am most grateful for everything I have learned here."

"That's O.K., Hideo. Have a nice day. He-he. Now, 'Flats.' "

The Question Party

"Yes, Maria, we will give the party on next Thursday night and I have an agreeable surprise in contemplation for all our old friends who may be here." The pleasant air about Mrs. Teach as she entered the parlor where her daughter was seated betokened the presence of something on her mind that gave her great satisfaction. The daughter had been importuning her mother for a party which after due deliberation she had decided to give and to make the evening more entertaining she had determined to introduce a new feature which she thought would create some excitement in the circle of her acquaintances and afford them the means of much amusement. She had just hit upon the plan before entering the room and the smile of satisfaction upon her face was noticed by her daughter.

"Shall we, Mother? I am so glad!" she answered. "But

what is it you are preparing for our friends? Are you going to sing?"

"No, Miss, I am going to do no such foolish thing! And, for your quizzing, you shall not know what it is until the evening of the party!"

"Now, Mother, that is too bad. You are too hardhearted. You know the extent of woman's curiosity and yet you will not gratify me. Are you going to introduce a new polka?"

"There is no use in your questioning; I shall not tell you anything about it, so you may as well save your breath."

"Do you intend showing your album quilt?" perseveringly inquired Maria.

"Now do not provoke me to cancel my promise by your pertinacity. I tell you as a punishment for quizzing your mother you shall not know until Thursday next what it is."

"Morning or evening, Mother?"

"Evening, Miss. So no more questions but get about writing your invitations."

Maria proceeded to the bookcase and taking from it her notepaper and envelopes commenced writing.

Eight o'clock on the evening of the party. The first who were ushered into the parlor were Mrs. Jawart and her two daughters, who were always the first at the reunions. The younger Miss Jawart was somewhere out of her teens, and the elder, although her face was profusely bedecked with curls—the original owner of which, being dead, had no further use for them—could not conceal that she was much older than she wished to be considered. Mr. and Mrs. White came next, the lady somewhat pompous in her manner, and the gentleman quite so. An interest in a canal boat had placed him, in his own view, among shipping merchants, and some of his acquaintances broadly hinted that if he were cut up in small pieces and retailed out for starch, he would be fulfilling his destiny. The two Misses Jennings and brother came next. These young ladies, the one eighteen and the other twenty, seemed somewhat disappointed, when they entered the room, at the absence of some of their young beaux, whom they expected to find there; this feeling was dispelled in a few moments, when a matched pair of the latter presented themselves.

Mr. Lynch, a bachelor of fifty, was the next to claim the attention of the company. He was a short, thickset man, with a small pair of whiskers that curled up on his cheekbones as if endeavoring to cultivate an acquaintance with his eyes. A few gray hairs in them, overlooked by the owner —his attention to them was exemplary—had been, in his toilet for the evening, elbowed, as it were, by the others to the fore, possibly to attract the attention of a few of the same color which peeped from behind the false hair of Miss Jawart. A standing collar formed a semi-wall around his neck, and shoes of the brightest polish graced his feet. At about half past nine, then, all the guests had assembled, filling comfortably both parlors and rendering the place vocal with their animated conversation.

The company had been engaged some time in singing when there was a call for a polka. In a few moments partners were selected and everyone was hopscotching through the figures at a lively rate, reminding one strongly of a group in a state of advanced intoxication. The mind of Maria suddenly became abstracted to such an extent by thoughts of the surprise that her mother had promised that she forgot her time and the dancers were compelled to stop and reprove her jokingly for her remissness. Just at that moment Mrs. Teach's voice could be heard, above the general din of laughter and music, calling for everyone, without exception, to come into the front parlor as she had something to show them which she thought would amuse. In her haste to get into the room Maria almost knocked one of the Misses Jennings over.

The company after much confusion being seated, Mrs. Teach took from the center table a handsome marble card basket containing a pack of plain, gilt-edged cards and explained that she had prepared an innocent and entertaining amusement for them which she hoped would prove interesting.

"Maria," she continued, "will you pass around this basket, my dear, and let each one of the company select from it one of the cards?"

Maria did as her mother requested.

"I shall propose a question," said Mrs. Teach, "to which each one must write an answer on the card they have. Which cards shall be placed in this vase on the pedestal behind me. After they are all deposited I will draw them out singly and will read them aloud. There is to be no mark upon the response by which its author may be known."

There was a general mustering of pencils at this announcement and an evident curiosity was immediately raised in regard to the subject which would be propounded.

"As there is a majority of ladies here, I shall propose for the first question: What is a bachelor?"

For the space of a quarter of an hour the pencils of the company made desperate attacks upon the faces of the cards which left them covered over with black lines. The last answer written and deposited in the vase, Mrs. Teach, with a smile, commenced the task of reading them aloud.

"*A target for fair hands to shoot at,*" she read.

A general laugh greeted this response.

"I beg of you, ladies," said Mr. Lynch, "not to shoot too close to me, but I know that my prayer is to no avail since your arrows are already in that vase."

The second card was drawn forth.

"*Any icy peak, on the mountain of humanity, that the sun of woman's love has never melted,*" read Mrs. Teach.

"Then I will nip you with my frost," said Mr. Lynch, putting his arms playfully around one of the Misses Jennings.

"How do you know it was my answer?" she cried, releasing herself from him.

"I read it in your face this moment," he replied.

"Then we must turn our faces from you, or we shall all betray ourselves, if you are such an excellent face reader," said the elder Miss Jawart.

"I beg you, do not!" exclaimed Mr. Lynch. "For that would deprive me of much pleasure."

"*An old maid's forlorn hope,*" said Mrs. Teach, reading the next response, the aptness of which was felt by all—yet a sense of propriety restrained any acknowledgment of this. Another card was instantly drawn to divert attention from it, and to relieve Miss Jawart from her unpleasant dilemma.

"*A fox longing for the grapes he pronounces sour.*"

"Now I really do object!" said Mr. Lynch. "I could never find it in my heart to pronounce any lady sour."

"Heart, indeed! This is the first time I ever knew you to acknowledge the possession of such an article," Mrs. Teach quickly replied.

"There you do me wrong, for, see! I have one now which you gave me," said Mr. Lynch, taking from his pocket a handsomely worked velvet heart. "And observe, there are as many pins in it as you are endeavoring to plant thorns in its partner here," he went on, placing his hand over that part of his coat which covered the real article.

The laugh was turned on Mrs. Teach and she drew forth another card.

"*A creature whose miseries might be pitied had he not the remedy within his reach.*"

"It must be you, Miss Bookly," said Mr. Lynch, "as you are sitting closest to me."

"I did not write it," said Miss Bookly. "And besides, Miss Jennings was sitting closest to you before she moved away after you put your arms around her.

"That is true," he said with a mock sigh.

Another card terminated the conversation on that subject.

"*Just like Mr. Lynch.*"

The merriment of the company knew no bounds at this answer. Mr. Lynch joined the rest with great zeal, and in a few moments exclaimed, "Well! I really do think you are making me a target to shoot at tonight. It is well for you that I am good-natured, else I might retaliate with some formulations of my own."

This is really a dumb game, thought Maria.

Mrs. Teach dipped into the vase for the next card.

"One who boasts of liberty but sighs for the slavery he condemns."

"That would be acute," Mr. Lynch said thoughtfully, "had I ever boasted. But I recall no such occasion. There is, in fact, a kind of shame and horror attached to the bachelor state—an odium combined with a tedium. Sleeping with strumpets is not the liveliest business in the world, I assure you."

"What are they like, really?" asked Miss Bookly.

"Some are choice, some are not," said Mr. Lynch.

"For heaven's sakes, man, be silent!" exclaimed Mr. White.

"A bit of fresh, as the expression runs," said Mr. Lynch, "can—"

Mr. White drew forth his pistol and shot Mr. Lynch dead with it.

"Good Lord! He is dead!" cried Mrs. Teach.

Dr. Balfour knelt over the body. "Yes, he is dead," he said. All assisted the Doctor in placing the carcass on the sofa.

"There is but one more card in the vase," said Mrs. Teach, peering into the article in question. "Dare we look at it?"

"Yes, yes," was the answer, in a subdued murmur.

"I sincerely hope that it may be a favorable one," said Mrs. Teach, "for I fear we have dealt harshly with our late friend tonight."

The last card was drawn from the vase. Mrs. Teach examined it closely on both sides and then proclaimed, "*Blank!*"

"A prophecy," said the younger Miss Jennings. "Who could have foreseen what was to happen?"

"It was not a matter of foreknowledge," said Maria. "The card is mine. I couldn't think of anything to write."

"Well," said Mrs. Teach, "I am not entirely satisfied with my little experiment this evening, and so shall leave it to another to choose the entertainment for our next."

"Not at all," said Mr. White. "The evening, despite its sad but necessary consequences, has been most delightful. I can't recall when more interesting things have been said or done, in all the years of my residence in this city. And as I shall have the pleasure of giving the next party, I shall most certainly adopt your little experiment, as you call it."

"What will the question be?" asked Miss Jawart.

"Something dangerous," said Mr. White, with a twinkle.

"Parties are always dangerous," said Miss Jawart.

"I am inviting Geronimo, chief of the Apache Indians, who happens to be in town," said Mr. White.

"That will make it all the more dangerous," said Mrs. Teach, "as I am told that he is extremely cruel to his enemies."

"He is extremely cruel to *everyone*," said Mr. White.

Yes, it was an agreeable party after all, Maria thought. My mother is not dumb. My mother is surprisingly intelligent. It was wrong of me to think ill of her. Now no one will ever know that Mr. Lynch was the man who— How strange is justice! How artful woman!

Author's note: This piece is an *objet trouvé*. It was originally published in *Godey's Lady's Book* in 1850, under the byline of a Hickory Broom. I have cut it and added some three dozen lines.

Belief

A group of senior citizens on a bench in Washington Square Park in New York City. There were two female senior citizens and two male senior citizens.

"Rabbit, rabbit, rabbit, rabbit," one of the women said suddenly. She turned her head to each of the four corners of an imaginary room as she did so.

The other senior citizens stared at her.

"Why did you do that?" one of the men asked.

"It's the first of the month. If you say 'rabbit' four times, once to each corner of the room, or the space that you are in, on the first of the month before you eat lunch, then you will be loved in that month."

Some angry black people walked by carrying steel-band instruments and bunches of flowers.

"I don't think that's true," the second woman senior citi-

75

zen said. "I never heard it before and I've heard everything."

"I think it's probably just an old wives' tale," one of the men said. The other male senior citizen cracked up.

"Shall we discuss *old men*?" the first woman asked the second woman.

The two men looked at the sky to make sure all of our country's satellites were in the right places.

"What about your daughter the nun?" the second woman, whose name was Elise, asked the first, whose name was Kate. "You haven't heard from her?"

"My daughter the nun," Kate said, "you wouldn't believe."

"Where is she?" Elise asked. "Georgia or somewhere, you told me but I forgot. Going to school you said."

"She's getting her master's," Kate said, "they send them. She's a rambling wreck from Georgia Tech. I was going down to visit at Thanksgiving."

"But you didn't."

"I called her and said I was coming and she said but Thanksgiving Day is the game. So I said the game, the game, O.K. I'll go to the game, I don't mind going to the game, get me a ticket. And she said but Mother I'm in the flash card section. My daughter the nun."

"They're different now," Elise said, "you're lucky she's not keeping company with one of those priests with his hair in a pigtail."

"Who can tell?" said Kate. "I'd be the last to know."

One of the men leaned around his partner and asked: "Well, is it working? Are you loved?"

"There was another thing we used to do," Kate said calmly. "You and your girl friend each wrote the names of three boys on three slips of paper, on the first day of the month. The names of three boys you wanted to ask you to go out with them. Then your girl friend held the three slips of paper in her cupped hands and you closed your eyes and picked—"

"I don't believe it," said the second male senior citizen, whose name was Jerome.

"You closed your eyes and picked one and put it in your shoe. And you did the same for her. And then that boy would come around. It always worked. Invariably."

"I don't believe it," Jerome said again. "I don't believe in things like that and never have. I don't believe in magic and I don't believe in superstition. I don't believe in Judaism, Christianity, or Eastern thought. None of 'em. I didn't believe in the First World War even though I was a child in the First World War and you'll go a long way before you find somebody who didn't believe in the First World War. That was a very popular war, where I lived. I didn't believe in the Second World War either and I was in it."

"How could you be in it if you didn't believe in it?" Elise asked.

"My views were not consulted," Jerome said. "They didn't ask me, they told me. But I still had my inner belief, which was that I didn't believe in it. I was in the MPs. I rose through the ranks. I was a provost marshal, at the end. I once shook down an entire battalion of Seabees, six hundred men."

"What is 'shook down'?"

"That's when you and your people go through their foot lockers and sea bags and personal belongings looking for stuff they shouldn't have."

"What shouldn't they have?"

"Black market stuff. Booze. Dope. Government property. Unauthorized weapons." He paused. "What else didn't I believe in? I didn't believe in the atom bomb but I was wrong about that. The unions."

"You were wrong about that too," said the other man, Frank. "I was a linotype operator when I was nineteen and I was a linotype operator until I was sixty and let me tell you, mister, if we hadn't had the union all we would have got was nickels and dimes. Nickels and dimes. Period. So don't say anything against the trade union movement while I'm sitting here, because I know what I'm talking about. You don't."

"I didn't believe in the unions and I didn't believe in the government whether Republican or Democrat," Jerome said. "And I didn't believe in—"

"The I.T.U. is considered a very good union," Elise said. "I once went with a man in the I.T.U. He was a composing-room foreman and his name was Harry Foreman, that was a coincidence, and he made very good money. We went to Luchow's a lot. He liked German food."

"Did you believe in the international Communist conspiracy?" Frank asked Jerome.

"Nope."

"You can't read," Frank said, "you're blind."

"Maybe."

"I haven't decided about whether there is an international Communist conspiracy," Elise said. "I'm still thinking about it."

"What's to think about?" Frank asked. "There was Czechoslovakia. Czechoslovakia says it all."

Some street people walked past the group of senior citizens but decided that the senior citizens weren't worth asking for small change. The decision was plain on their faces.

"When I was a girl, a little girl, I had to go into my father's bar to get the butter," Kate said. "My father had a bar in Brooklyn. The icebox was in the bar. The only icebox. My mother sent me downstairs to get the butter. All the men turned and looked at me as I entered the bar."

"But your father bounded out from behind the bar and got you the butter meanwhile looking sternly at all the other people in the bar to keep them from looking at you," Elise suggested.

"No," Kate said. "He was on his ass most of the time. What they say about bartenders not drinking is not true."

"Also I didn't believe in the United Nations and before that I didn't believe in the League of Nations," Jerome said. "Furthermore," he said, giving Kate a meaningful glance, "I didn't believe women should be given the vote."

Kate gazed at Jerome's coat, which was old, at his shirt, old, then at his pants, which were quite old, and at his shoes, which were new.

"Do you have prostate trouble?" she asked.

"Yes," Jerome said, with a startled look. "Of course. Why?"

"Good," Kate said. "I don't believe in prostate trouble. I don't believe there is such a thing as a prostate."

She gave him a generous and loving smile.

"You mean to tell me that if you put the piece of paper with the boy's name on it in your shoe on the first day of the month he *invariably* came around?" Elise asked Kate.

"Invariably," Kate said. "Without fail. Worked every time."

"Goddamn," Elise said. "Wish I'd known that."

"There was one thing I believed," Jerome said.

"What?"

"It's religious."

"What is it?"

"My pal the rabbi told me, he's dead now. He said it was a Hasidic writing."

"So?" said Elise. "So, so, so?"

"It is forbidden to grow old."

The old people thought about this for a while, on the bench.

"It's good," Kate said. "I could do without the irony."

"Me too," Elise said. "I could do without the irony."

"Maybe it's not so good?" Jerome asked. "What do you think?"

"No," Kate said. "It's good." She gazed about her at the new life sprouting in sandboxes and jungle gyms. "Wish I had some kids to yell at."

Tales of
the Swedish Army

Suddenly, turning a corner, I ran into a unit of the Swedish Army. Their vehicles were parked in orderly rows and filled the street, mostly six-by-sixes and jeeps, an occasional APC, all painted a sand color quite different from the American Army's dark green. To the left of the vehicles, on a big school playground, they had set up two-man tents of the same sand color, and the soldiers, blond red-faced men, lounged about among the tents, making not much noise. It was strange to see them there, I assumed they were on their way to some sort of joint maneuvers with our own troops. But it was strange to see them there.

I began talking to a lieutenant, a young, pleasant man; he showed me a portable chess clock he'd made himself, which was for some reason covered in matchstick bamboo painted purple. I told him I was building an addition to the rear of my house, as a matter of fact I had with me a carpenter's level I'd just bought, and I showed him that. He said he had some free time, and asked if I needed help. I suggested that probably his unit would be moving out fairly soon, but he waved a hand to indicate that their departure was not imminent. He seemed genuinely interested in assisting me, so I accepted.

His name was Bengt and he was from Uppsala. I'd been there so we talked about Uppsala, then about Stockholm and Bornholm and Malmö. I asked him if he knew the work of the Swedish poet Bodil Malmsten; he didn't. My house (not really mine, my sister's, but I lived there and paid rent) wasn't far away, we stood in the garden looking up at the rear windows on the parlor floor, I was putting new ones in. So I climbed the ladder and he began handing me up one of the rather heavy prefab window frames, and my hammer slid from the top of the ladder and fell and smashed into his chess clock, which he'd carefully placed on the ground, against the wall.

I apologized profusely, and Bengt told me not to worry, it didn't matter, but he kept shaking the chess clock and turning it over in his hands, trying to bring it to life. I rushed down the ladder and apologized again, and looked at it myself, both dials were shattered and part of the purple matchstick casing had come off. He said again not to worry, he could fix it, and that we should get on with the job.

After a while Bengt was up on the ladder tacking the new frames to the two-by-fours with sixteen-penny nails. He was very skillful and the work was going quickly; I was standing in the garden steadying the ladder as he was sometimes required to lean out rather far. He slipped and tried to recover, and bashed his face against the wall, and broke his nose.

He stood in the garden holding his nose with both hands, the hands as if clasped in prayer over his nose. I apologized profusely. I ran into the house and got some ice cubes and paper towels and told him I'd take him to the hospital right away but he shook his head and said no, they had doctors of their own. I wanted to do something for him so I took him in and sat him down and cooked him some of my fried chicken, which is rather well-known although the secret isn't much of a secret, just lots of lemon-pepper marinade and then squeezing fresh lemon juice over it just before serving. I could see he was really very discouraged about his nose and I had to keep giving him fresh paper towels but he complimented me very highly on the chicken and gave me a Swedish recipe for chicken stuffed with parsley and butter and stewed, which I wrote down.

Then Bengt told me various things about the Swedish Army. He said that it was a tough army and a sober one, but small; that everybody in the army pretty well knew everybody else, and that they kept their Saab jets in deep caves that had been dug in the mountains, so that if there was a war, nothing could happen to them. He said that the part I'd seen was just his company, there were two more plus a heavy-weapons company bivouacking at various spots in the city, making up a full battalion. He said the soldiers were mostly Lutherans, with a few Presbyterians and Evangelicals, and that drugs were not a problem but that people sometimes overslept, driving the sergeants crazy. He said that the Swedish Army was thought to have the best weapons in the world, and that they kept them very clean. He said that he probably didn't have to name their principal potential enemy, because I knew it already, and that the army-wide favorite musical group was Abba, which could sometimes be seen on American television late at night.

By now the table was full of bloody towels and some blood had gotten on his camouflage suit, which was in three shades of green and brown. Abruptly, with a manly gesture, Bengt informed me that he had fallen in love with my sister. I said that was very curious, in that he had never met her. "That is no difficulty," he said, "I can see by looking around this house what kind of a woman she must be. Very tall, is she not? And red hair, is that not true?" He went on describing my sister, whose name is Catherine, with a disturbing accuracy and increasing enthusiasm, correctly identifying her as a teacher and, furthermore, a teacher of painting. "These are hers," he said, "they must be," and rose to inspect some oils in Kulicke frames on the walls. "I knew it. From these, dear friend, a great deal can be known of the temperament of the painter, his or her essential spirit. I will divorce my wife immediately," he said, "and marry Catherine as soon as it is legally possible." "You're already married!" I said, and he hung his head and admitted yes, that it was so. But in Sweden, he said, many people were married to each other who, for one reason or another, no longer loved each other . . . I said that happened in our own country too, many cases personally known to me, and that if he wished to marry Catherine I would not stand in his way, but would, on the contrary, do everything in my power to further the project. At this moment the bell rang; I answered it and Catherine entered with her new husband, Richard.

I took Bengt back to his unit in a cab, one hand clutching his nose, the other his heart, the remains of his chess clock in his lap. We got there just in time, a review was in progress, the King of Sweden was present, a handsome young man in dress uniform with a silver sword, surrounded by aides similarly clad. A crowd had gathered and Bengt's company paraded by, looking vastly trim and efficient in their polished boots and red berets, and a very pretty little girl came out of the crowd and shyly handed the King a small bouquet of flowers. He bent graciously to accept them, beautiful small yellow roses, and a Rocky Mountain spotted-fever tick leaped from a rose and bit him on the cheek. I was horrified, and the King slapped his cheek and swore that the Swedish Army would never come to visit us again.

The Abduction
from the Seraglio

I was sitting in my brand-new Butler building, surrounded by steel of high quality folded at ninety-degree angles. The only thing prettier than ladies is an I-beam painted bright yellow. I told 'em I wanted a big door. A big door in front where a girl could hide her car if she wanted to evade the gaze of her husband the rat-poison salesman. You ever been out with a rat-poison salesman? They are fine fellows with little red eyes.

I was playing with my forty-three-foot overhead traveling crane which is painted bright yellow. I was practicing knocking over the stepladder with the hook. I was at a low point. I'd been thinking about bread, colored steel bread, all kinds of colors of steel bread—red yellow purple green brown steel bread—then I thought no, that's not it. And I'd already made all the welded-steel four-thousand-pound artichokes the world could accommodate that week, and they wouldn't let me drink no more, only a little Lone Star beer now and then which I don't much care for. And my new Waylon Jennings record had a scratch on it, went crack crack crack across the whole width of Side One. It was the kind of impasse us creative people reach every Thursday, some prefer other days. So I figured that in order not to totally waste this valuable time of my life, I had better get on the stick and bust Constanze out of the seraglio.

> *Chorus:*
> Oh Constanze oh Constanze
> What you doin' in that se-rag-li-o?
> I been poppin' Darvon and mothballs
> Poppin' Darvon and mothballs
> Ever since I let you go.

Well, I motored out to the seraglio, got blindsided on the Freeway by two hundred thousand guys trying to get home from their work at the rat-poison factories, all two hundred thousand tape decks playin' the same thing, some kind of roll-on-down-the-road song

> rollin'
> rollin'
> rollin'
> rollin'

but there wasn't just a hell of a lot of actual forward motion despite this hymn to possibility. The seraglio turned out to be a Butler building too, much like mine only vaster of course, that son of a bitch. I spent a little while admiring that fine red-painted steel that you can put the pieces together of out of a catalogue and set her down on your slab and be barbecuing your flank steak from the A. & P. by five o'clock on the same day. The Pasha didn't have any great big doors in his, just one little tee-ninesy door with a picture of an unfed-recently Doberman pasted on it, I took that as a hint and I thought Constanze, Constanze, how could you be so dumb?

The thing is, and I hate to admit it, Constanze's a little dumb. She's not so dumb as a lady I once knew who thought the Mark of Zorro was an N, but she's not perfect. You tell her you heard via the jungle drums that there's a vacancy in Willie Jake Johnson's bed and her eyes will cut to the side just for a moment, which means she's thinking. She's not conservative. I'm some kind of an artist, but I'm conservative. Mine is the art of the possible, plus two. She, on the contrary, spent many years as a talented and elegant country-music groupie. She knows things I do not know. Happy dust is $1,900 an ounce now, I hear tell—she's tasted it, I haven't. It's a small thing, but irritating. She's dumb in what she knows, if you follow me.

> *Chorus:*
> Oh Constanze oh Constanze
> What you doin' in that se-rag-li-o?
> I been sleepin' on paper towels
> Sleepin' on paper towels and
> Drinkin' Sea & Ski
> Ever since I let you go.

The Pasha is a Plymouth dealer, actually. He has this mysterious power over people and events which is called ten million dollars a year, gross. About the only thing we share in the way of common humanity is four welded-steel artichokes, which he bought right from the studio, which is where he saw Constanze. The artichoke is a beautiful form, maybe too mannerly, I roughen mine up some, that's where the interest is. I don't even mind the damn Plymouth, as a form, but what I can't stand is a dealer. In anything. I know that this is a small picky-minded dumb-ass prejudice, but it's been earned. Anyhow the Pasha, as we call him, noticed that Constanze was some beautiful, in fact semi-incredible looking, with black hair. He turned her head, as used to be said. He'd got to the left of flank steak, and he employed that. If we're having Neiman-Marcus time, I can't compete. (In all honesty I have to concede that he is fairly handsome, for a Pasha, and excels in a number of expensive sports.) He put her in a Butler building just to mock me and because she's not so dumb she'd be caught dead in a big fancy layout in River Oaks or somewhere She's got values. What I'm trying to suggest is, she's in a delicate relation to the real.

I can't understand this. She is so great. When we go partying she always takes care to dance with Bill Cray's four-year-old girl, who's a fool for dancing. She made me read *War and Peace*, which struck me at first glance as terrible thick. She renews my subscription to the *Texas Observer* every year. She contributes regularly to the United Way and got gassed in great cities a time or two while expressing her opinion of the recent war. She's kind to rat-poison salesmen. She's afraid of the dark. She took care of me that time I had my little psychotic episode. She is so great. Once I saw her slug a guy in a supermarket who was whacking his kid, his legal right, with undue enthusiasm. The really dreadful thought, to me, is that her real might be the real one.

Well, I opened the door. The Doberman came at me raging and snarling and generally carrying on in the way he felt was expected of him. I threw him a fifty-five-pound reinforced-concrete pork chop which knocked him silly. I spoke to Constanze. We used to walk down the street together bumping our hipbones together in joy, before God and everybody. I wanted to float in the air again some feeling of that. It didn't work. I'm sorry. But I guess, as the architects say, there's no use crying over spilt marble. She will undoubtedly move on and up and down and around in the world, New York, Chicago, and Temple, Texas, making everything considerably better than it was, for short periods of time. We adventured. That's not bad.

> Chorus:
> Oh Constanze oh Constanze
> What you doin' in that se-rag-li-o?
> How I miss you
> How I miss you

The Death of
Edward Lear

The death of Edward Lear took place on a Sunday morning in May 1888. Invitations were sent out well in advance. The invitations read:

> Mr. Edward LEAR
> *Nonsense Writer and Landscape Painter*
> *Requests the Honor of Your Presence*
> *On the Occasion of His DEMISE.*
> San Remo   2:20 *a.m.*
> *The 29th of May*   *Please reply*

One can imagine the feelings of the recipients. Our dear friend! is preparing to depart! and such-like. Mr. Lear! who has given us so much pleasure! and such-like. On the other hand, his years were considered. Mr. Lear! who must be, now let me see . . . And there was a good deal of, I remember the first time I (dipped into) (was seized by) . . . But on the whole, Mr. Lear's acquaintances approached the occasion with a mixture of solemnity and practicalness, perhaps remembering the words of Lear's great friend, Tennyson:

> Old men must die,
> or the world would grow mouldy

and:

> For men may come and men may go,
> But I go on forever.

People prepared to attend the death of Edward Lear as they might have for a day in the country. Picnic baskets were packed (for it would be wrong to expect too much of Mr. Lear's hospitality, under the circumstances); bottles of wine were wrapped in white napkins. Toys were chosen for the children. There were debates as to whether the dog ought to be taken or left behind. (Some of the dogs actually present at the death of Edward Lear could not restrain themselves; they frolicked about the dying man's chamber, tugged at the bedclothes, and made such nuisances of themselves that they had to be removed from the room.)

Most of Mr. Lear's friends decided that the appropriate time to arrive at the Villa would be midnight, or in that neighborhood, in order to allow the old gentleman time to make whatever remarks he might have in mind, or do whatever he wanted to do, before the event. Everyone understood what the time specified in the invitation meant. And so, the visitors found themselves being handed down from their carriages (by Lear's servant Giuseppe Orsini) in almost total darkness. Pausing to greet people they knew, or to corral straying children, they were at length ushered into a large room on the first floor, where the artist had been accustomed to exhibit his watercolors, and thence by a comfortably wide staircase to a similar room on the second floor, where Mr. Lear himself waited, in bed, wearing an old velvet smoking jacket and his familiar silver spectacles with tiny oval lenses. Several dozen straight-backed chairs had been arranged in a rough semicircle around the bed; these were soon filled, and later arrivals stood along the walls.

Mr. Lear's first words were: "I've no money!" As each new group of guests entered the room, he repeated, "I've no money! No money!" He looked extremely tired, yet calm. His ample beard, gray yet retaining patches of black, had evidently not been trimmed in some days. He seemed nervous and immediately began to discourse, as if to prevent anyone else from doing so.

He began by thanking all those present for attending and expressing the hope that he had not put them to too great an inconvenience, acknowledging that the hour was "an unusual one for visits!" He said that he could not find words sufficient to disclose his pleasure in seeing so many of his friends gathered together at his side. He then delivered a pretty little lecture, of some twelve minutes' duration, on the production of his various writings, of which no one has been able to recall the substance, although everyone agreed that it was charming, graceful, and wise.

He then startled his guests with a question, uttered in a kind of shriek: "Should I get married? Get married? Should I marry?"

Mr. Lear next offered a short homily on the subject Friendship. Friendship, he said, is the most golden of the affections. It is also, he said, often the *strongest* of human ties, surviving strains and tempests fatal to less sublime relations. He noted that his own many friendships constituted the richest memory of a long life.

A disquisition on Cats followed.

When Mr. Lear reached the topic Children, a certain restlessness was observed among his guests. (He had not ceased to shout at intervals, "Should I get married?" and "I've no money!") He then displayed copies of his books, but as everybody had already read them, not more than a polite interest was generated. Next he held up, one by one, a selection of his watercolors, views of various antiquities and picturesque spots. These, too, were familiar; they were the same watercolors the old gentleman had been offering for sale, at £5 and £10, for the past forty years.

Mr. Lear now sang a text of Tennyson's in a setting of his own, accompanying himself on a mandolin. Although his voice was thin and cracked frequently, the song excited vigorous applause.

Finally he caused to be hauled into the room by servants

an enormous oil, at least seven feet by ten, depicting Mount Athos. There was a murmur of appreciation, but it did not seem to satisfy the painter, for he assumed a very black look.

At 2:15 Mr. Lear performed a series of actions the meaning of which was obscure to the spectators.

At 2:20 he reached over to the bedside table, picked up an old-fashioned pen which lay there, and died. A death mask was immediately taken. The guests, weeping unaffectedly, moved in a long line back to the carriages.

People who had attended the death of Edward Lear agreed that, all in all, it had been a somewhat tedious performance. Why had he seen fit to read the same old verses, sing again the familiar songs, show the well-known pictures, run through his repertoire once more? Why invitations? Then something was understood: that Mr. Lear had been doing what he had always done and therefore, not doing anything extraordinary. Mr. Lear had transformed the extraordinary into its opposite. He had, in point of fact, created a gentle, genial misunderstanding.

Thus the guests began, as time passed, to regard the affair in an historical light. They told their friends about it, reenacted parts of it for their children and grandchildren. They would reproduce the way the old man had piped "I've no money!" in a comical voice, and quote his odd remarks about marrying. The death of Edward Lear became so popular, as time passed, that revivals were staged in every part of the country, with considerable success. The death of Edward Lear can still be seen, in the smaller cities, in versions enriched by learned interpretation, textual emendation, and changing fashion. One modification is curious; no one knows how it came about. The supporting company plays in the traditional way, but Lear himself appears shouting, shaking, vibrant with rage.

Concerning
the Bodyguard

Does the bodyguard scream at the woman who irons his shirts? Who has inflicted a brown burn on his yellow shirt purchased expensively from Yves St. Laurent? A great brown burn just over the heart?

Does the bodyguard's principal make conversation with the bodyguard, as they wait for the light to change, in the dull gray Citroën? With the second bodyguard, who is driving? What is the tone? Does the bodyguard's principal comment on the brown young women who flock along the boulevard? On the young men? On the traffic? Has the bodyguard ever enjoyed a serious political discussion with his principal?

Is the bodyguard frightened by the initials D.I.T.?

Is the bodyguard frightened by the initials C.N.D.?

Will the bodyguard be relieved, today, in time to see the

film he has in mind—*Emmanuelle Around the World?* If the bodyguard is relieved in time to see *Emmanuelle Around the World*, will there be a queue for tickets? Will there be students in the queue?

Is the bodyguard frightened by the slogan *Remember 17 June?* Is the bodyguard frightened by black spray paint, tall letters ghostly at the edges, on this wall, on this wall? At what level of education did the bodyguard leave school?

Is the bodyguard sufficiently well-paid? Is he paid as well as a machinist? As well as a foreman? As well as an army sergeant? As well as a lieutenant? Is the Citroën armored? Is the Mercedes armored? What is the best speed of the Mercedes? Can it equal that of a BMW? A BMW motorcycle? Several BMW motorcycles?

Does the bodyguard gauge the importance of his principal in terms of the number of bodyguards he requires? Should there not be other cars leading and following his principal's car, these also filled with bodyguards? Are there sometimes such additional precautions, and does the bodyguard, at these times, feel himself part of an ocean of bodyguards? Is he exalted at these times? Does he wish for even more bodyguards, possibly flanking cars to the right and left and a point car far, far ahead?

After leaving technical school, in what sort of enterprises did the bodyguard engage before accepting his present post? Has he ever been in jail? For what sort of offense? Has the bodyguard acquired a fondness for his principal? Is there mutual respect? Is there mutual contempt? When his principal takes tea, is the bodyguard offered tea? Beer? Who pays?

Can the bodyguard adduce instances of professional success?

Had he a previous client?

Is there a new bodyguard in the group of bodyguards? Why?

How much does pleasing matter? What services does the bodyguard provide for his principal other than the primary one? Are there services he should not be asked to perform? Is he nevertheless asked from time to time to perform such services? Does he refuse? Can he refuse? Are there, in addition to the bodyguard's agreed-upon compensation, tips? Of what size? On what occasions?

In the restaurant, a good table for his principal and the distinguished gray man with whom he is conferring. Before it (between the table with the two principals and the door), a table for the four bodyguards. What is the quality of the conversation between the two sets of bodyguards? What do they talk about? Soccer, perhaps, Holland vs. Peru, a match which they have all seen. Do they rehearse the savaging of the Dutch goalkeeper Piet Schrijvers by the bastard Peruvian? Do they discuss Schrijvers's replacement by the brave Jan Jongbloed, and what happened next? Has the bodyguard noted the difference in quality between his suit and that of his principal? Between his shoes and those of his principal?

In every part of the country, large cities and small towns, bottles of champagne have been iced, put away, reserved for a celebration, reserved for a special day. Is the bodyguard aware of this?

Is the bodyguard tired of waking in his small room on the

Calle Caspe, smoking a Royale Filtre, then getting out of bed and throwing wide the curtains to discover, again, eight people standing at the bus stop across the street in postures of depression? Is there on the wall of the bodyguard's small room a poster showing Bruce Lee in a white robe with his feet positioned in such-and-such a way, his fingers outstretched in such-and-such a way? Is there a rosary made of apple beads hanging from a nail? Is there a mirror whose edges have begun to craze and flake, and are there small blurrish Polaroids stuck along the left edge of the mirror, Polaroids of a woman in a dark-blue scarf and two lean children in red pants? Is there a pair of dark-blue trousers plus a long-sleeved white shirt (worn once already) hanging in the dark-brown wardrobe? Is there a color foldout of a naked young woman torn from the magazine VIR taped inside the wardrobe door? Is there a bottle of Long John Scotch atop the cheese-colored mini-refrigerator? Two-burner hotplate? Dull-green ceramic pot on the windowsill containing an unhealthy plant? A copy of *Explication du Tai Chi*, by Bruce Tegner? Does the bodyguard read the newspaper of his principal's party? Is he persuaded by what he reads there? Does the bodyguard know which of the great blocs his country aligned itself with during the Second World War? During the First World War? Does the bodyguard know which countries are the preeminent trading partners of his own country, at the present time?

Seated in a restaurant with his principal, the bodyguard is served, involuntarily, turtle soup. Does he recoil, as the other eats? Why is this near-skeleton, his principal, of such importance to the world that he deserves six bodyguards, two to a shift with the shifts changing every eight hours, six bodyguards of the first competence plus supplementals on occasion, two armored cars, stun grenades ready to hand under the front seat? What has he meant to the world? What are his plans?

Is the retirement age for bodyguards calculated as it is for other citizens? Is it earlier, fifty-five, forty-five? Is there a pension? In what amount? Those young men with dark beards staring at the Mercedes, or staring at the Citroën, who are they? Does the bodyguard pay heed to the complaints of his fellow bodyguards about the hours spent waiting outside this or that Ministry, this or that Headquarters, hours spent propped against the fenders of the Mercedes while their principal is within the (secure) walls? Is the thick glass of these specially prepared vehicles thick enough? Are his fellow bodyguards reliable? Is the new one reliable?

Is the bodyguard frightened by young women of good family? Young women of good family whose handbags contain God knows what? Does the bodyguard feel that the situation is *unfair?* Will the son of the bodyguard, living with his mother in a city far away, himself become a bodyguard? When the bodyguard delivers the son of his principal to the school where all of the children are delivered by bodyguards, does he stop at a grocer's on the way and buy the child a peach? Does he buy himself a peach?

Will the bodyguard, if tested, be equal to his task? Does the bodyguard know which foreign concern was the successful bidder for the construction of his country's nuclear reprocessing plant? Does the bodyguard know which sections of the National Bank's yearly report on debt service have been falsified? Does the bodyguard know that the general amnesty of April coincided with the rearrest of sixty persons? Does the bodyguard know that the new, liberalized press laws of May were a provocation? Does the bodyguard patronize a restaurant called the Crocodile? A place packed with young, loud, fat Communists? Does he spill a drink, to disclose his spite? Is his gesture understood?

Are the streets full of stilt-walkers? Stilt-walkers weaving ten feet above the crowd in great papier-mâché bird heads, black and red costumes, whipping thirty feet of colored cloth above the heads of the crowd, miming the rape of a young female personage symbolizing his country? In the Mercedes, the bodyguard and his colleague stare at the hundreds, men and women, young and old, who move around the Mercedes, stopped for a light, as if it were a rock in a river. In the rear seat, the patron is speaking into a telephone. He looks up, puts down the telephone. The people pressing around the car cannot be counted, there are too many of them; they cannot be known, there are too many of them; they cannot be predicted, they have volition. Then, an opening. The car accelerates.

Is it the case that, on a certain morning, the garbage cans of the city, the garbage cans of the entire country, are overflowing with empty champagne bottles? Which bodyguard is at fault?

The Zombies

In a high wind the leaves fall from the trees. The zombies are standing about talking. "Beautiful day!" "Certainly is!" The zombies have come to buy wives from the people of this village, the only village for miles around that will sell wives to zombies. "Beautiful day!" "Certainly is!" The zombies have brought many cattle. The bride-price to a zombie is exactly twice that asked of an ordinary man. The cattle are also zombies and the zombies are in terror lest the people of the village understand this.

These are good zombies. Gris Grue said so They are painted white all over. Bad zombies are unpainted and weep with their noses, their nostrils spewing tears The village chief calls the attention of the zombies to the fine brick buildings of the village, some of them one thousand bricks high—daughters peering from the windows, green plants in some windows and, in others, daughters. "You must promise not to tell the Bishop," say the zombies, "promise not to tell the Bishop, beautiful day, certainly is."

The white-painted zombies chatter madly, in the village square, in an impersonation of gaiety. "Bought a new coat!" "You did!" "Yes, bought a new coat, this coat I'm wearing, I think it's very fine!" "Oh it is, it is, yes I think so!" The cattle kick at the chain-link fence of the corral. The kiss of a dying animal, a dying horse or dog, transforms an ordinary man into a zombie. The owner of the ice-cream shop has two daughters. The crayfish farmer has five daughters, and the captain of the soccer team, whose parents are dead, has a sister. Gris Grue is not here. He is away in another country, seeking a specific for deadly nightshade. A zombie with a rectal thermometer is creeping around in the corral, under the bellies of the large, bluish-brown animals. Someone says the Bishop has been seen riding in his car at full speed toward the village.

If a bad zombie gets you, he will weep on you, or take away your whiskey, or hurt your daughter's bones. There are too many daughters in the square, in the windows of the buildings, and not enough husbands. If a bad zombie gets you, he will scratch your white paint with awls and scarifiers. The good zombies skitter and dance. "Did you see that lady? Would that lady marry me? I don't know! Oh what a pretty lady! Would that lady marry me? I don't know!" The beer distributor has set up a keg of beer in the square. The local singing teacher is singing. The zombies say: "Wonderful time! Beautiful day! Marvelous singing! Excellent beer!

Would that lady marry me? I don't know!" In a high wind the leaves fall from the trees, from the trees.

The zombie hero Gris Grue said: "There are good zombies and bad zombies, as there are good and bad ordinary men." Gris Grue said that many of the zombies known to him were clearly zombies of the former kind and thus eminently fit, in his judgment, to engage in trade, lead important enterprises, hold posts in the government, and participate in the mysteries of Baptism, Confirmation, Ordination, Marriage, Penance, the Eucharist, and Extreme Unction. The Bishop said no. The zombies sent many head of cattle to the Bishop. The Bishop said, everything but Ordination. If a bad zombie gets you, he will create insult in your bladder. The bad zombies banged the Bishop's car with a dead cow, at night. In the morning the Bishop had to pull the dead zombie cow from the windscreen of his car, and cut his hand. Gris Grue decides who is a good zombie and who is a bad zombie; when he is away, his wife's mother decides. A zombie advances toward a group of thin blooming daughters and describes, with many motions of his hands and arms, the breakfasts they may expect in a zombie home.

"Monday!" he says. "Sliced oranges boiled grits fried croakers potato croquettes radishes watercress broiled spring chicken batter cakes butter syrup and café au lait! Tuesday! Grapes hominy broiled tenderloin of trout steak French-fried potatoes celery fresh rolls butter and café au lait! Wednesday! Iced figs Wheatena porgies with sauce tartare potato chips broiled ham scrambled eggs French toast and café au lait! Thursday! Bananas with cream oat-meal broiled patassas fried liver with bacon poached eggs on toast waffles with syrup and café au lait! Friday! Straw-berries with cream broiled oysters on toast celery fried perch lyonnaise potatoes cornbread with syrup and café au lait! Saturday! Muskmelon on ice grits stewed tripe herb ome-lette olives snipe on toast flannel cakes with syrup and café au lait!" The zombie draws a long breath. "Sunday!" he says. "Peaches with cream cracked wheat with milk broiled Spanish mackerel with sauce maître d'hôtel creamed chicken beaten biscuits broiled woodcock on English muffin rice cakes potatoes à la duchesse eggs Benedict oysters on the half shell broiled lamb chops pound cake with syrup and café au lait! And imported champagne!" The zombies look anxiously at the women to see if this prospect is pleasing.

A houngan (zombie-maker) grasps a man by the hair and forces his lips close to those of a dying cat. If you do heavy labor for a houngan for ten years, then you are free, but still a zombie. The Bishop's car is working well. No daughter of this village has had in human memory a true husband, or anything like it. The daughters are tired of kissing each other, although some are not. The fathers of the village are tired of paying for their daughters' sewing machines, lowboys, and towels. A bald zombie says, "Oh what a pretty lady! I would be nice to her! Yes I would! I think so!" Bad zombies are leaning against the walls of the buildings, watching. Bad zombies are allowed, by law, to mate only with sheep ticks. The women do not want the zombies, but zombies are their portion. A woman says to another woman: "These guys are zombies!" "Yes," says the second woman, "I saw a handsome man, he had his picture in the paper, but he is not here." The zombie in the corral finds a temperature of a hundred and ten degrees.

The villagers are beating upon huge drums with mops. The Bishop arrives in his great car with white episcopal flags flying from the right and left fenders. "Forbidden, forbidden, forbidden!" he cries. Gris Grue appears on a silver sled and places his hands over the Bishop's eyes. At the moment of sunset the couples, two by two, are wed. The corral shudders as the cattle collapse. The new wives turn to their new husbands and say: "No matter. This is what we must do. We will paste photographs of the handsome man in the photograph on your faces, when it is time to go to bed. Now let us cut the cake." The good zombies say, "You're welcome! You're very welcome! I think so! Undoubtedly!" The bad zombies place sheep ticks in the Bishop's car. If a bad zombie gets you, he will scarify your hide with chisels and rakes. If a bad zombie gets you, he will make you walk past a beautiful breast without even noticing.

Morning

—Say you're frightened. Admit it.

—In Colorado, by the mountains. In California, by the sea. Everywhere, by breaking glass.

—Say you're frightened. Confess.

—Timid as a stag. They've got a meter wired to my sheet, I don't know what it measures. I get a dollar a night. When I wake suddenly, I notice it's there. I watch my hand aging, sing a little song.

—Were you invited to the party?

—Yes, I was. Stood there smiling. I thought, Those are tight pants, how kind of her. Wondered if she was orange underneath. What shall we do? Call up Mowgli? Ask him over? Do you like tongue? Sliced? With mushrooms? Is it a private matter? Is Scriabin as smart as he looks? This man's a fool—why are you talking to him? Yes, his clothes are interesting, but inside are dull bones.

—This gray light, I don't see how you stand it.

—A firestorm of porn all around—orange images, dunes and deserts. Bursts of quarreling through the walls. I wonder who the people are? I tried that Cuisine Minceur, didn't like it. Oh, it looks pretty—

—Say you're frightened.

—I'm frightened. By flutes and flower girls and sirens. We get a lot of sirens because of the hospital. By coffee, dead hanging plants, people who think too fast, vestments and bells.

—Get some Vitamin E. I take eight hundred units.

—The sound of glass breaking. I thought, Oh Christ, not again. The last time they got a bicycle, fancy Japanese bicycle somebody'd left in the hall. We changed the lock. Guy left his crowbar. Actually it wasn't a crowbar it was a jack handle.

—I'm not afraid of crime, there's got to be crime, it's the manner or mode that— I mean if they could just take it out of your bank account, by punching a few buttons or something . . .

—I'm not afraid of snakes. There was a snake-handling bunch where we spent the summers. I used to go to their meetings now and again, do a little handling.

—Not afraid of the mail, not so much as I used to be, all those threatening letters, I just say sticks and stones, sticks and stones, see the triage nurse.

—It's only when you stop to think about it. I don't stop.

—Not afraid of hurricanes because we used to have

them, where I lived, not afraid of tarantulas, used to have them too, they jump, have to chop them up with a hoe, long-handled hoe as opposed to the stoop hoe, by preference.

—Nature in general not seen as antipathetic. Nor are other people, except for those who want to slap your ears back without first presenting their carefully reasoned, red-white-and-blue threats.

—Behavior in general a wonderful sea, in which we can swim, or leap, or stumble.

—She got out of bed and, doing a cute little walk, walked to the bathroom. I dreaded the day I would see her real walk.

—There's the sunset gun. That means we can loosen up and get friendly. Think we can get any of that government money?

—I sent for the forms. Merrily merrily merrily merrily.

—Think we can get us some of that good per diem?

—If you decide to run for it a bus is better. No one's seated facing you. They've got bigger windows now, and the drivers are usually reliable.

—Well that's one thing I want to stay away from. Flight, I mean. Too much like defeat.

—But when I get to all these strange places they seem empty. Nobody on the streets and I'm not used to that. Their restaurants all have the same things: filet, surf 'n' turf, prime rib. Spend a few days in a hotel and then check out, leaving a dollar or two for the maids.

—Turkeying around trying to get situated.

—Searching the room for someone to go to bed with. What if she agrees?

—That's happened to me several times. You just have to be honest.

—The love of gain is insatiable. This is true.

—What are you afraid of? Mornings, noons, or nights?

—Mornings. I send out a lot of postcards.

—Take a picture of this exceptionally dirty window. Its grays. I think I can get you a knighthood, I know a guy. What about the Eternal Return?

—Distant, distant, distant. Thanks for calling Jim it was good to talk to you.

—They played "One O'Clock Jump," "Two O'Clock Jump," "Three O'Clock Jump," and "Four O'Clock Jump." They were very good. I saw them on television. They're all dead now.

—That scare you?

—Naw that doesn't scare me.

—That scare you?

—Naw that doesn't scare me.

—What scares you?

—My hand scares me. It's not well.

—Hear that? That's wolf talk. Not bad is it?

—Scarcely had I reloaded when a black rhinoceros, a female as it proved, stood drinking at the water.

—Let me give you a hint: *Find me one animal that is capable of personal friendship.*

—So I decided it was about time we got gay. I changed the record, that helped, and fiddled with the lights—

—Call up Bomba the Jungle Boy? Get his input?

—Fixed up the Kool-Aid with some stuff I had with me.

Complicated the decor with carefully placed items of lawn furniture, birdbaths, sundials, mirrored globes on stands . . .

—That set toes to tapping, did it?

—They were pleased. We danced Inventions & Sinfonias. It wasn't bad. It was a success.

—It is this that the new portraits are intended to celebrate.

—Then, out of another chute, the bride appeared, caracoling and sunfishing across the arena.

—I knew her. I was very fond of her. I am very fond of her. I wish them well.

—As do I. She's brave.

—Think we can get some of that fine grant money?

—If we can make ourselves understood. If I applaud, the actors understand that I am pleased. If I take a needle and singe it with a match, you understand that I have picked up a splinter in my foot. If I say "Have any of the English residents been murdered?," you understand that I am cognizant of native unrest. If I hand you two copies of a thesis bound in black cloth, you understand that I am trying to improve myself. Appeals to patriotism, small-boat warnings up.

—Say you're frightened.

—I'm frightened. But maybe not tomorrow.

—Well that's one thing I want to stay away from. You can get mad instead. I got mad, really got mad.

—Put-on anger. A technique of managers.

—Got so mad I coulda bit a chisel in two.

—And very graciously. Skin of dreams, paint marks, red

scratches, grass stains. We watched 60 *Minutes*. Fed on ixias, wild garlic, the core of aloes, gum of acacias. She's gone now, took an early plane. How do I feel? O.K.

—Another bright glorious day. How do you feel? Have you tried to get a drink on one of these new trains? It's as easy as pie. Have you got anything we could put over the windows? Tarpaper or maybe some boards? Do you want to hear "The Battle Hymn of the Republic"? Is there any more of this red?

—Jugs and jugs. Two weeks would do it, two weeks in a VW Rabbit.

—Going home.

—No, thank you.

—You're afraid of it?

—Indeed, do I still live?

—What are you afraid of?

—One old man alone in a room. Two old men alone in a room. Three old men alone in a room.

—Well maybe you could talk to them or something.

—And say: Howdy, have you heard about pleasure, have you heard about fun? Let's go out and bust up a bar, it's been a long time. What are you up to, what are your plans? Still lifting weights? I've been screwing all night, how 'bout you? "You please me, happiness!"

—Well I don't think about this stuff a lot of the time.

—Humility is barefoot, Lewdness is physically attractive and holds a sprig of colewort, the Hour is a wheel, and Courage is strangling a lion, by shoving a mailed fist down its throat.

—How did the party end?

—I wasn't there. Got to scat, I said, got to get away, got to creep, it's that time of night. Matthew, Mark, Luke, and John, bless the bed that I lie on.

—Say you're frightened.

—Less and less. I have a smoke detector and tickets to everywhere. I have a guardian angel blind from birth and a packet of Purple-top White Globe turnip seeds, for the roof.

—Want to see my collection of bass clarinets? Want to see my collection of painters' ears? This gray light, I don't see how you stand it.

—I grayed it up myself. Sets off the orange.

—A fine person. Took the Fire Department exam and passed it. That's just one example.

—All women are mortal, she explained to me, and Caius is a woman.

—Say you're not frightened. Inspire me.

—After a while, darkness, and they give up the search.

On the Steps
of the Conservatory

—C'mon Hilda don't fret.

—Well Maggie it's a blow.

—Don't let it bother you, don't let it get you down.

—Once I thought they were going to admit me to the Conservatory but now I know they will never admit me to the Conservatory.

—Yes they are very particular about who they admit to the Conservatory. They will never admit you to the Conservatory.

—They will never admit me to the Conservatory, I know that now.

—You are not Conservatory material I'm afraid. That's the plain truth of it.

—You're not important, they told me, just remember

that, you're not important, what's so important about you? What?

—C'mon Hilda don't fret

—Well Maggie it's a blow.

—When are you going to change yourself, change your self into a loaf or a fish?

—Christian imagery is taught at the Conservatory, also Islamic imagery and the imagery of Public Safety.

—Red, yellow, and green circles.

—When they told me I got between the poles of my rickshaw and trotted heavily away.

—The great black ironwork doors of the Conservatory barred to you forever.

—Trotted heavily away in the direction of my house. My small, poor house.

—C'mon Hilda don't fret.

—Yes, I am still trying to get into the Conservatory, although my chances are probably worse than ever.

—They don't want pregnant women in the Conservatory.

—I didn't tell them, I lied about it.

—Didn't they ask you?

—No they forgot to ask me and I didn't tell them.

—Well then it's hardly on that account that—

—I felt they knew.

—The Conservatory is hostile to the new spirit, the new spirit is not liked there.

—Well Maggie it's a blow nevertheless. I had to go back to my house.

—Where although you entertain the foremost artists and intellectuals of your time you grow progressively more despondent and depressed.

—Yes he was a frightful lawyer.

—Lover?

—That too, frightful. He said he could not get me into the Conservatory because of my unimportance.

—Was there a fee?

—There's always a fee. Pounds and pounds.

—I stood on the terrace at the rear of the Conservatory and studied the flagstones reddened with the lifebloods of generations of Conservatory students. Standing there I reflected: Hilda will never be admitted to the Conservatory.

—I read the Conservatory Circular and my name was not among those listed.

—Well I suppose it was in part your espousal of the new spirit that counted against you.

— I will never abjure the new spirit.

—And you're a veteran too, I should have thought that would have weighed in your favor.

—Well Maggie it's a disappointment, I must admit that frankly.

—C'mon Hilda don't weep and tear your hair here where they can see you.

—Are they looking out of the windows?

—Probably they're looking out of the windows.

—It's said that they import a cook, on feast days.

—They have naked models too.

—Do you really think so? I'm not surprised.

—The best students get their dinners sent up on trays.

—Do you really think so? I'm not surprised.

—Grain salads and large portions of choice meats.

—Oh it hurts, it hurts, it hurts.

—Bread with drippings, and on feast days cake.

—I'm as gifted as they are, I'm as gifted as some of them.

—Decisions made by a committee of ghosts. They drop black beans or white beans into a pot.

—Once I thought I was to be admitted. There were encouraging letters.

—You're not Conservatory material I'm afraid. Only the best material is Conservatory material.

—I'm as good as some of those who rest now in the soft Conservatory beds.

—Merit is always considered closely.

—I could smile back at the smiling faces of the swift, dangerous teachers.

—Yes, we have naked models. No, the naked models are not emotionally meaningful to us.

—I could work with clay or paste things together.

—Yes, sometimes we paste things on the naked models —clothes, mostly. Yes, sometimes we play our Conservatory violins, cellos, trumpets for the naked models, or sing to them, or correct their speech, as our deft fingers fly over the sketch pads . . .

—I could I suppose fill out another application, or several.

—Yes, you have considerable of a belly on you now. I remember when it was flat, flat as a book.

—I will die if I don't get into the Conservatory, die.

—Naw you won't you're just saying that.

—I will completely croak if I don't get into the Conservatory, I promise you.

—Things are not so bad, you can always do something else, I don't know what, c'mon Hilda be reasonable.

—My whole life depends on it.

—Oh God I remember when it was flat. Didn't we tear things up, though? I remember running around that town, and hiding in dark places, that was a great town and I'm sorry we left it.

—Now we are grown, grown and proper.

—Well, I misled you. The naked models are emotionally meaningful to us.

—They are?

—We love them and sleep with them all the time— before breakfast, after breakfast, during breakfast.

—Why that's all right!

—Why that's rather neat!

—I like that!

—That's not so bad!

—I wish you hadn't told me that.

—C'mon Hilda don't be so single-minded, there are lots of other things you can do if you want.

—I guess they operate on some kind of principle of exclusivity. Keeping some people out while letting other people in.

—We got a Coushatta Indian in there, real full-blooded Coushatta Indian.

—In there?

—Yes. He does hanging walls out of scraps of fabric and twigs, very beautiful, and he does sand paintings and plays on whistles of various kinds, sometimes he chants, and he bangs on a drum, works in silver, and he's also a weaver, and he translates things from Coushatta into English and from English into Coushatta and he's also a crack shot and can bulldog steers and catch catfish on trotlines and ride bareback and make medicine out of common ingredients, aspirin mostly, and he sings and he's also an actor. He's very talented.

—My whole life depends on it.

—Listen Hilda maybe you could be an Associate. We have this deal whereby you pay twelve bucks a year and that makes you an Associate. You get the Circular and have all the privileges of an Associate.

—What are they?

—You get the Circular.

—That's all?

—Well I guess you're right.

—I'm just going to sit here I'm not going to go away.

—Your distress is poignant to me.

—I'll have the baby right here right on these steps.

—Well maybe there'll be good news one of these days.

—I feel like a dead person sitting in a chair.

—You're still pretty and attractive.

—That's good to hear I'm pleased you think that.

—And warm you're warm you're very warm.

—Yes I have a warm nature very warm.

—Weren't you in the Peace Corps also years ago?

—I was and drove ambulances too down in Nicaragua.

—The Conservatory life is just as halcyon as you imagine it—precisely so.

—I guess I'll just have to go back to my house and clean up, take out the papers and the trash.

—I guess that kid'll be born one of these days, right?

—Continue working on my études no matter what they say.

—That's admirable I think.

—The thing is not to let your spirit be conquered.

—I guess that kid'll be born after a while, right?

—I guess so. Those boogers are really gonna keep me out of there, you know that?

—Their minds are inflexible and rigid.

—Probably because I'm a poor pregnant woman don't you think?

—You said you didn't tell them.

—But maybe they're very shrewd psychologists and they could just look at my face and tell.

—No it doesn't show yet how many months are you?

—Two and a half just about you can tell when I take my clothes off.

—You didn't take your clothes off did you?

—No I was wearing you know what the students wear. Jeans and a sarape. I carried a green book bag.

—Jam-packed with études.

—Yes. He asked where I had gotten my previous training and I told him.

—Oh boy I remember when it was flat, flat as the deck of something, a boat or a ship.

—You're not important, they told me.

—Oh sweetie I am so sorry for you.

—We parted then I walking through the gorgeous Conservatory light into the foyer and then through the great black ironwork Conservatory doors.

—I was a face on the other side of the glass.

—My aspect as I departed most dignified and serene.

—Time heals everything.

—No it doesn't.

—Cut lip fat lip puffed lip split lip.

—Haw! haw! haw! haw!

—Well Hilda there are other things in life.

—Yes Maggie I suppose there are. None that I want.

—Non-Conservatory people have their own lives. We Conservatory people don't have much to do with them but we are told they have their own lives.

—I suppose I could file an appeal if there's anywhere to file an appeal to. If there's anywhere.

—That's an idea we get stacks of appeals, stacks and stacks.

—I can wait all night. Here on the steps.

—I'll sit with you. I'll help you formulate the words.

—Are they looking out of the windows?

—Yes I think so. What do you want to say?

—I want to say my whole life depends on it. Something like that.

—It's against the rules for Conservatory people to help non-Conservatory people you know that.

—Well Goddammit I thought you were going to help me.

—Okay. I'll help you. What do you want to say?

—I want to say my whole life depends on it. Something like that.

—We got man naked models and woman naked models, harps, giant potted plants, and drapes. There are hierarchies, some people higher up and others lower down. These mingle, in the gorgeous light. We have lots of fun. There's lots of green furniture you know with paint on it. Worn green paint. Gilt lines one-quarter inch from the edges. Worn gilt lines.

—And probably flambeaux in little niches in the walls, right?

—Yeah we got flambeaux. Who's the father?

—Guy named Robert.

—Did you have a good time?

—The affair ran the usual course. Fever, boredom, trapped.

—Hot, rinse, spin dry.

—Is it wonderful in there Maggie?

—I have to say it is. Yes. It is.

—Do you feel great, being there? Do you feel wonderful?

—Yes, it feels pretty good. Very often there is, upon the tray, a rose.

—I will never be admitted to the Conservatory.

—You will never be admitted to the Conservatory.

—How do I look?

—Okay. Not bad. Fine.

—I will never get there. How do I look?

—Fine. Great. Time heals everything Hilda.

—No it doesn't.

—Time heals everything.

—No it doesn't. How do I look?

—Moot.

The Leap

—Today we make the leap to faith. Today.

—Today?

—Today.

—We're really going to do it? At last?

—Spent too much time fooling around. Today we do it.

—I don't know. Maybe we're not ready?

—I am cheered by the wine of possibility and the growing popularity of light. Today's the day.

—You're serious.

—Intensely. First, we examine our consciences.

—I am a double-minded man. Have always been a double-minded man.

—Each examining his own conscience, rooting out, naming, remembering and re-experiencing every last little cank and wrinkle. Root and branch.

—Smiting each conscience hip and thigh.

—Thigh and hip. Smite! Smite!

—God is good and we are but poor wretches who—

—Wait.

—Poor slovening wretches who but for the goodness of God would—

—Wait. This will be painful, you know. A bit.

—Oh my God.

—What?

—I just had a thought.

—A prick of conscience.

—Yes. Item 34.

—What's Item 34?

—An unkindness. One of a series. Series long as your arm.

—You list them separately.

—Yes.

—You don't just throw them all together into a great big trash bag labeled—

—No. I sweat each one. Seriatim.

—I said it would be painful.

—Might we postpone it?

—Meditate instead on His works? Their magnificence.

—Not that we could in a hundred million years exhaust—

—It's a sort of if-a-bird-took-one-grain-of-sand-and-flew-all-his-life-and-then-another-bird-took-another-grain-of-sand-and-flew-all-his-life situation.

—Contemplate only the animals. Restrict the field.

'Course we got over a million species, so far. New ones being identified every day. Insects, mostly.

—I like plants better than animals.

—Animals give you a lot of warmth. A dog would be an example.

—I like people better than plants, plants better than animals, paintings better than animals, and music better than animals.

—Praising the animals, then, would not be your first impulse.

—I *respect* the animals. I *admire* the animals. But could we contemplate something else?

—Take a glass of water, for example. A glass of water is a miraculous thing.

—The blue of the sky, against which we find the shocking green of the leaves of the trees.

—The trees. "I think that I shall never see slash A poem lovely as a tree."

—"A tree whose hungry mouth is prest slash Against the earth's sweet flowing breast."

—Why "mouth"?

—Why "breast"?

—The working of the creative mind.

—An unfathomable mystery.

—Never to be fathomed.

—I wouldn't even want to fathom it. If one fathomed it, who can say what frightful things might thereupon be fathomed?

—Fathoming such is beyond the powers of poor ravening noodles like ourselves, who but for the—

—And another thing. The human voice.

—My God you're right. The human voice.

—Bessie Smith.

—Alice Babs.

—Joan Armatrading.

—Aretha Franklin.

—Each voice testifying to the greater honor and glory of God, each in its own way.

—Damn straight.

—Sweet Emma Barrett the Bell Gal.

—Got you.

—*Das Lied von der Erde.*

—I couldn't agree more.

—Then there are the bad things. Cancer.

—An unfathomable mystery, at this point. But one which must inevitably succumb to the inexorable forward march of scientific progress.

—Economic inequality.

—In my view, this will be ameliorated in the near future by the pressure of population growth. Pressure of population growth being such that economic inequality simply cannot endure.

—What about Z.P.G.?

—An ideal rather than a social slash political reality.

—So God's creatures, in your opinion, multiplying and multiplying and multiplying as per instruction, will—

—Propagate fiercely until the sum total of what has been propagated yields a pressure so intense that every feature great or small of every life great or small is instantly scrutinized weighed judged decided upon and disposed of by the sum total of one's peers in doubtless electronic ongoing all-seeing everlasting congress assembled. Thus if one guy has a little advantage, a little edge, it is instantly taken away from him and similarly if another guy has a little lack, some little lack, this little lack is instantly supplied, by the arbiters. Things cannot be otherwise. Because there's not going to be any room to fucking *move*, man, do you follow me? there's not going to be any room to fucking *sneeze*, without you're sneezing *on* somebody . . .

—This is the Divine plan?

—Who can know the subtle workings of His mind? But it seems to be the way events are—

—That's another thing. The human mind.

—Good God yes. The human mind.

—The human mind which is in my judgment the finest of our human achievements.

—Much the finest. I can think of nothing remotely comparable.

—Is a flower, however beautiful and interesting, comparable to the human mind? I think not.

—Matter of higher and lower levels of complexity.

—I concur. This is not to knock the flower.

—This is not to say that the beautiful, interesting flower is not, in its own terms, entirely fantastic

—The toast of the earth. Did I ever tell you about that time when I was in Korea and Cardinal Spellman came to see us at Christmas and his plane was preceded by another plane broadcasting sacred music over the terrain? Spraying the terrain as it were with sacred music?

—So that those on earth could hear and be edified.

—"O Little Town of Bethlehem "

—Yes, the human mind deserves the greatest respect. Not so good of course as the Divine mind, but not bad.

—Leibniz. William of Ockham. Maimonides. The Vienna Circle. The Frankfurt School. Manichaeus. Peirce. Occasionalism. A pretty array. I believe Occasionalism's been discredited. But let it stand. It was a nice try, and philosophy, as my dear teacher taught me so long long ago, is not to be regarded as a graveyard of dead systems.

—The question of suicide. Self-slaughter. Maybe we ought to think about it?

—What's to think about?

—Look at this.

—What is it?

—The bill.

—For what is it the bill?

—A try.

—Whose?

—An acquaintance.

—Good God.

—Yes.

—Ought two slash twenty-four electrocardiogram ought two ought ought ought ought one, thirty-five bucks.

—Ought two slash twenty-four cardiopulmonary two ought ought ought ought ought one, forty bucks.

—Ought two slash twenty-four inhalation therapy one four ought ought ought ought one, sixty bucks.

—Ought two slash twenty-four room four nine one five, a neat one-eighty.

—It goes on for miles.

—What's the total?

—Shade under two thousand. Nineteen hundred and two dollars and ninety cents.

—You'd think they'd give you the ninety cents.

—You'd think they would.

—And the acquaintance?

—She's well.

—This being an example of the leap away from faith.

—Exactly. You can jump either way.

—Shall we examine our consciences now?

—You are mad with hurry.

—We are but poor lapsarian futiles whose preen glands are all out of whack and who but for the grace of God's goodness would—

—Do you think He wants us to grovel quite so much?

—I don't think He gives a rap. But it's traditional.

—We hang by a slender thread.

—The fire boils below us.

—The pit. Crawling with roaches and other things.

—Tortures unimaginable, but the worst the torture of knowing it could have been otherwise, had we shaped up.

—Purity of heart is to will one thing.

—No. Here I differ with Kierkegaard. Purity of heart is, rather, to will several things, and not know which is the better, truer thing, and to worry about this, forever

—A continuing itch of the mind.

—Sometimes assuagable by timely masturbation.

—I forgot. Love.

—Oh my God, yes. Love. Both human and divine.

—Love, the highest form of human endeavor.

—Coming or going, the absolute zenith.

—Is it *permitted* to differ with Kierkegaard?

—Not only permitted but necessary. If you love him.

—Love, which is a kind of permission to come closer than ordinary norms of good behavior might usually sanction.

—Back rubs.

—Which enables us to see each other without clothes on, for example, in lust and shame.

—Examining perfections, imperfections.

—Which allows us to say wounding things to each other which would not be kosher under the ordinary rules of civilized discourse.

—Walkin' my baby back home.

—Love which allows us to live together male and female in small grubby apartments that would only hold one sane person, normally.

—Misting the plants together—the handsome, talented plants.

—He who hath not love is a sad cookie.

—This is the way, walk ye in it. Isaiah 30:21.

—Can't make it, man.

—What?

—I can't make it

—The leap

—Can't make it I am a double-minded man.

—Well

—An incorrigibly double-minded man.

—What then?

—Keep on trying?

—Yes. We must.

—Try again another day?

—Yes. Another day when the plaid cactus is watered, when the hare's-foot fern is watered.

—Seeds tingling in the barrens and veldts.

—Garden peas yellow or green wrinkling or rounding.

—Another day when locust wings are baled for shipment to Singapore, where folks like their little hit of locust-wing tea.

—A jug of wine. Then another jug.

—The Brie-with-pepper meeting the toasty loaf.

—Another day when some eighty-four-year-old guy complains that his wife no longer gives him presents.

—Small boys bumping into small girls, purposefully.

—Cute little babies cracking people up.

—Another day when somebody finds a new bone that proves we are even ancienter than we thought we were.

—Gravediggers working in the cool early morning.

—A walk in the park.

—Another day when the singing sunlight turns you every way but loose.

—When you accidentally notice the sublime.

—Somersaults and duels.

—Another day when you see a woman with really red hair. I mean really red hair.

—A wedding day.

—A plain day.
—So we'll try again? Okay?
—Okay.
—Okay?
—Okay.

Great Days

—When I was a little girl I made mud pies, dangled strings down crayfish holes hoping the idiot crayfish would catch hold and allow themselves to be hauled into the light. Snarled and cried, ate ice cream and sang "How High the Moon." Popped the wings off crickets and floated stray Scrabble pieces in ditch water. All perfect and ordinary and perfect.

—Featherings of ease and bliss.

—I was preparing myself. Getting ready for the great day.

—Icy day with salt on all the sidewalks.

—Sketching attitudes and forming pretty speeches.

—Pitching pennies at a line scraped in the dust.

—Doing and redoing my lustrous abundant hair.

—Man down. Center and One Eight.

—Tied flares to my extremities and wound candy canes into my lustrous, abundant hair. Getting ready for the great day.

—For I do not deny that I am a little out of temper.

—Glitches in the system as yet unapprehended.

—Oh that clown band. Oh its sweet strains.

—Most excellent and dear friend. Who the silly season's named for.

—My demands were not met. One, two, three, four.

—I admire your dash and address. But regret your fear and prudence.

—Always worth making the effort, always.

—Yes that's something we do. Our damnedest. They can't take that away from us.

—The Secretary of State cares. And the Secretary of Commerce.

—Yes they're clued in. We are not unprotected. Soldiers and policemen.

—Man down. Corner of Mercer and One Six.

—Paying lots of attention. A clear vision of what can and can't be done.

—Progress extending far into the future. Dams and aqueducts. The amazing strength of the powerful.

—Organizing our deepest wishes as a mother foresightedly visits a store that will be closed tomorrow.

—Friendship's the best thing.

—One of the best things. One of the very best.

—I performed in a hall. Alone under the burning lights.

—The hall ganged with admiring faces. Except for a few.

—Julia was there. Rotten Julia.

—But I mean you really like her don't you?

—Well I mean who doesn't like violet eyes?

—Got to make the effort, scratch where it itches, plans, schemes, directives, guidelines.

—Well I mean who doesn't like frisky knees?

—Yes she's lost her glow. Gone utterly.

—The strains of the city working upon an essentially non-urban sensibility.

—But I love the city and will not hear it traduced.

—Well, me too. But after all. But still.

—Think Julia's getting it on with Bally.

—Yeah I heard about that he's got a big mouth.

—But handsome hip bones got to give him that.

—I remember, I can feel them still, pressing into me as they once did on hot afternoons and cool nights and feverish first-thing-in-the-mornings.

—Yes, Bally is a regal memory for everyone.

—My best ghost. The one I think about, in bitter times and good.

—Trying to get my colors together. Trying to play one off against another. Trying for cancellation.

—I respect your various phases. Your sweet, even discourse.

—I spent some time away and found everyone there affable, gentle, and good.

—Nonculminating kind of ultimately affectless activity.

—Which you mime so gracefully in auditoria large and small.

—And yet with my really wizard! good humor and cheerful thoughtless mien, I have caused a lot of trouble.

—I suppose that's true. Strictly speaking.

—Bounding into the woods on all fours barking like a mother biting at whatever moves in front of me—

—Do you also save string?

—On my free evenings and paid holidays. Making the most of the time I have here on this earth. Knotting, sewing, weaving, welding.

—Naming babies, Lou, Lew, Louis.

—And his toes, wonderful toes, that man has got toes.

—Decorated with rings and rubber bands.

—Has a partiality for white. White gowns, shifts, aprons, flowers, sauces.

—He was a salty dog all right. Salty dog.

—I was out shooting with him once, pheasant, he got one, with his fancy shotgun. The bird bursting like an exploding pillow.

—Have to stand there and watch them, their keen eyes scanning the whatever. And then say "Good shot!"

—Oh I could have done better, better, I was lax.

—Or worse, don't fret about it, could have put your cute little butt in worse places, in thrall to dismaler personalities.

—I was making an effort. What I do best.

—You are excellent at it. Really first-rate.

—Never fail to knock myself out. Put pictures on the walls and pads under the rugs.

—I really admire you. I really do. To the teeth.

—Bust your ass, it's the only way.

—As we learn from studying the careers of all the great figures of the past. Heraclitus and Launcelot du Lac.

—Polish the doorknobs with Brasso and bring in the sea bass in its nest of seaweed.

—And not only that. And not only that.

—Tickling them when they want to be tickled. Abstaining, when they do not.

—Large and admirable men. Not neglecting the small and ignoble. Dealing evenhandedly with every situation on a case-by-case basis.

—Yeah yeah yeah yeah yeah.

—Knew a guy wore his stomach on his sleeve. I dealt with the problem using astrology in its medical aspects. His stomach this, his stomach that, God Almighty but it was tiresome, tiresome in the extreme. I dealt with it by using astrology in its medical aspects.

—To each his own. Handmade bread and individual attention.

—You've got to have something besides yourself. A cat, too often.

—I could have done better but I was dumb. When you're young you're sometimes dumb.

—Yeah yeah yeah yeah yeah. I remember.

—Well let's have a drink.

—Well I don't mind if I do.

—I have Goldwasser, Bombay gin and Old Jeb.

—Well I wouldn't mind a Scotch myself.

—I have that too.

—Growing older and with age, less beautiful.

—Yeah I've noticed that. Losing your glow.

—Just gonna sit in the wrinkling house and wrinkle. Get older and worse.

—Once you lose your glow you never get it back.

—Sometimes by virtue of the sun on a summer's day.

—Wrinkling you so that you look like a roast turkey.

—As is the case with the Oni of Ife. Saw him on television.

—Let me show you this picture.

—Yes that's very lovely. What is it?

—It's "Vulcan and Maia."

—Yes. He's got his hooks into her. She's struggling to get away.

—Vigorously? Vigorously. Yes.

—Who's the artist?

—Spranger.

—Never heard of him.

—Well.

—Yes, you may hang it. Anywhere you like. On that wall or that wall or that wall.

—Thank you.

—Probably I can get ahead by working hard, paying attention to detail.

—I thought that. Once I thought that.

—Reading a lot of books and having good ideas.

—Well that's not bad. I mean it's a means.

—Do something wonderful. I don't know what.

—Like a bass player plucking the great thick strings of his instrument with powerful plucks.

—Blood vessels bursting in my face just under the skin all the while.

—Hurt by malicious criticisms all very well grounded.

—Washing and rewashing my lustrous, abundant hair.

—For Leatherheart, I turn my back. My lustrous, abundant back.

—That cracks them up does it?

—At least they know I'm in town.

—Ease myself into bed of an evening brain jumping with hostile fluids.

—It's greens in a pot.

—It's confetti in the swimming pool.

—It's U-joints in the vichyssoise.

—It's staggers under the moon.

—He told me terrible things in the evening of that day as we sat side by side waiting for the rain to wash the watercolors from his watercolor paper. Waiting for the rain to wash the paper clean, quite clean.

—Took me by the hand and led me through all the rooms. Many rooms.

—I know all about it.

—The kitchen is especially splendid.

—Quite so.

—A dozen Filipinos with trays.

—Close to that figure.

—Trays with edibles. Wearables. Readables. Collectibles.

—Ah, you're a fool. A damned fool.

—Goodbye, madame. Dip if you will your hand in the holy water font as you leave, and attend as well to the poor box just to the right of the door.

—Figs and kiss-me-nots. I would meet you upon this honestly.

—I went far beyond the time normally allotted for a speaker. Far.

—In Mexico City. Wearing the black jacket with the silver conchos. And trousers of fire pink.

—Visited a health club there, my rear looked like two pocketbooks, they worked on it.

—You were making an effort.

—Run in the mornings too, take green tea at noon, study household management, finance, repair of devices.

—Born with a silver hoe in your mouth.

—Yes. Got to get going, got to make some progress.

—Followed by development of head banging in the child.

—I went far beyond the time normally allotted to, or for, a speaker. It is fair to say they were enthralled. And transfixed. Inappropriate laughter at some points but I didn't mind that.

—Did the Eminence arrive?

—In a cab. In his robes of scarlet.

—He does a tough Eminence.

—Yes very tough. I was allowed to kiss the ring. He sat there, in the audience, just like another member of the audience. Just like anybody. Transfixed and enthralled.

—Whirling and jigging in the red light and throwing veils on the floor and throwing gloves on the floor—

—One of my finest. They roared for ten minutes.

—I am so proud of you. Again and again. Proud of you.

—Oh well, yes. I agree. Quite right. Absolutely.

—What? Are you sure? Are you quite sure? Let me show you this picture.

—Yes that's quite grand. What is it?

—It's "Tancred Succored by Ermina."

—Yes she's sopping up the blood there, got a big rag, eems a sweet girl, God he's out of it isn't he, dead or dying horse at upper left . . . Who's the artist?

—Ricchi.

—Never heard of him.

—Well.

—I'll take it. You may stack it with the others, against hat wall or that wall or that wall—

—Thank you. Where shall I send the bill?

—Send it anywhere you like. Anywhere your little heart desires.

—Well I hate to be put in this position. Bending and subservient.

—Heavens! I'd not noticed. Let me raise you up.

—Maybe in a few days. A few days or a few years.

—Lave you with bee jelly and bone oil.

—And if I have ever forgiven you your astonishing successes—

—Mine.

—And if I have ever been able to stomach your serial triumphs—

—The sky. A rectangle of gray in the foreground and behind that, a rectangle of puce. And behind that, a square of silver gilt.

—Got to get it together, get the big bucks.

—Yes I'm thinking hard, thinking hard.

—Frolic and detour.

—What's that mean?

—I don't know just a bit of legal language I picked up somewhere.

—Now that I take a long look at you—

—In the evening by the fireside—

—I find you utterly delightful. Abide with me. We'll have little cakes with smarm, yellow smarm on them—

—Yes I just feel so fresh and free here. One doesn't feel that way every day, or every week.

—Last night at two the barking dog in the apartment above stopped barking. Its owners had returned. I went into the kitchen and barked through the roof for an hour. I believe I was understood.

—Man down. Corner of Water and Eight Nine.

—Another wallow?

—I've wallowed for today thank you. Control is the thing.

—Control used to be the thing. Now, abandon.

—I'll never achieve abandon.

—Work hard and concentrate. Try Clown, Baby, Hell-hag, Witch, the Laughing Cavalier. The Lord helps those—

—Purple bursts in my face as if purple staples had been stapled there every which way—

—Hurt by malicious criticisms all very well grounded—

—Oh that clown band. Oh its sweet strains.

—The sky. A rectangle of glister. Behind which, a serene brown. A yellow bar, vertical, in the upper right.

—I love you, Harmonica, quite exceptionally.

—By gum I think you mean it. I think you do.

—It's "Portia Wounding Her Thigh."

—It's "Wolfram Looking at His Wife Whom He Has mprisoned with the Corpse of Her Lover."

—If you need a friend I'm yours till the end.

—Your gracious and infinitely accommodating presence.

—Julia's is the best. Best I've ever seen. The finest.

—The muscle of jealousy is not in me. Nowhere.

—Oh it is so fine. Incomparable.

—Some think one thing, some another.

—The very damn best believe me.

—Well I don't know, I haven't seen it.

—Well, would you like to see it?

—Well, I don't know, I don't know her very well do /ou?

—Well, I know her well enough to ask her.

—Well, why don't you ask her if it's not an incon-/enience or this isn't the wrong time or something.

—Well, probably this is the wrong time come to think of t because she isn't here and some time when she is here would probably be a better time.

—Well, I would like to see it right now because just ralking about it has got me in the mood to see it. If you know what I mean.

—She told me that she didn't like to be called just for hat purpose, people she didn't know and maybe wouldn't ike if she did know, I'm just warning you.

—Oh.

—You see.

—I see.

—I could have done better. But I don't know how. Could have done better, cleaned better or cooked better or. I don't know. Better.

—You smile. And the angels sing. La la la la la la la la la la la la.

—Blew it. Blew it.

—Had a clown at the wedding he officiated standing there in his voluptuous white costume his drum and trumpet at his feet. He said, "Do you, Harry . . ." and all that. The guests applauded, the clown band played, it was a brilliant occasion.

—Our many moons of patience and accommodation. Tricks and stunts unknown to common cunts.

—The guests applauded. Above us, a great tent with red and yellow stripes.

—The unexploded pillow and the simple, blunt sheet.

—I was fecund, savagely so.

—Painting dead women by the hundreds in passionate imitation of Delacroix.

—Sailing after lunch and after sailing, gin.

—Do not go into the red barn, he said. I went into the red barn. Julia. Swinging on a rope from hayloft to tack room. Gazed at by horses with their large, accepting eyes. They somehow looked as if they knew.

—You packed hastily reaching the station just before midnight counting the pennies in your purse.

—Yes. Regaining the city, plunged once more into activities.

—You've got to have something besides yourself. A cause, interest, or goal.

—Made myself knowledgeable in certain areas, one, two, three, four. Studied the Value Line and dipped into cocoa.

—The kind of thing you do so well.

—Acquired busts of certain notables, marble, silver, bronze. The Secretary of Defense and the Chairman of the Joint Chiefs.

—Wailed a bit now and then into the ears of friends and caverns of the telephone.

—But I rallied. Rallied.

—Made an effort. Made the effort.

—To make soft what is hard. To make hard the soft. To conceal what is black with use, under new paint. Check the tomatoes with their red times, in the manual. To enspirit the spiritless. To get me a jug and go out behind the barn sharing with whoever is out behind the barn, peasant or noble.

—Sometimes I have luck. In plazas or taverns.

—Right as rain. I mean okey-dokey.

—Unless the participant affirmatively elects otherwise.

—What does that mean?

—Damfino. Just a bit of legal language I picked up somewhere.

—You are the sunshine of my life.

—Toys toys I want more toys.

—Yes, I should think you would.

—That wallow in certainty called the love affair.

—The fading gray velvet of the sofa. He clowned with my panties in his teeth. Walked around that way for half an hour.

—What's this gunk here in this bucket?

—Bread in milk, have some.

—I think I could eat a little something.

—A mistletoe salad we whipped up together.

—Stick to it, keep after it. Only way to go is all the way.

—Want to buy a garter belt? Have one, thanks. Cut your losses, try another town, split for the tall timber.

—Well it's a clean afternoon, heavy on the azaleas.

—Yes they pride themselves on their azaleas. Have competitions, cups.

—I dashed a hope and dimmed an ardor. Promises shimmering like shrimp in light just under the surface of the water.

—Peered into his dental arcade noting the health of his pink tissue.

—Backed into a small table which overturned with a scattering of ashtrays and back copies of important journals.

—What ought I to do? What do you advise me? Should I try to see him? What will happen? Can you tell me?

—Yes it's caring and being kind. We have corn dodgers too and blood sausage.

—Lasciviously offered a something pure and white.

—But he hastily with an embarrassed schottische of the hands covered you up again.

—Much like that. Every day. I don't mind doing the work if I get the results.

—We had a dog because we thought it would keep us together. A plain dog.

—Did it?

—Naw it was just another of those dumb ideas we had we thought would keep us together.

—Bone ignorance.

—Saw him once more, he was at a meeting I was at, had developed an annoying habit of coughing into his coat collar whenever he—

—Coughed.

—Yes he'd lift his coat collar and cough into it odd mannerism very annoying.

—Then the candles going out one by one—

—The last candle hidden behind the altar—

—The tabernacle door ajar—

—The clapping shut of the book.

—I got ready for the great day. The great day came, several times in fact.

—Each time with memories of the last time.

—No. These do not in fact intrude. Maybe as a slight shimmer of the over-and-done-with. Each great day is itself, with its own war machines, rattles, and green lords. There is the hesitation that the particular day won't be what it is meant to be. Mostly it is. That's peculiar.

—He told me terrible things in the evening of that day as we sat side by side waiting for the rain to wash his watercolor paper clean. Waiting for the rain to wash the watercolors from his watercolor paper.

—What do the children say?

—There's a thing the children say.

—What do the children say?

—They say: Will you always love me?

—Always.

—Will you always remember me?

—Always.

—Will you remember me a year from now?

—Yes, I will.

—Will you remember me two years from now?

—Yes, I will.

—Will you remember me five years from now?

—Yes, I will.

—Knock knock.

—Who's there?

—You see?